BIG&bold

From the publisher of *BeadStyle* magazine

KALMBACH BOOKS

26

46

Kalmbach Books
21027 Crossroads Circle
Waukesha, Wisconsin 53186
www.Kalmbach.com/Books

Published in 2009
13 12 11 10 09   1 2 3 4 5

Manufactured in the United States of
America

ISBN: 978-0-87116-286-1

The material in this book has appeared
previously in *BeadStyle* magazine.
BeadStyle is registered as a trademark.

**Publisher's Cataloging-in-
Publication Data**

Big & bold : how to make dramatic
  beaded jewelry / from the publishers of
  Beadstyle Magazine.
    p. : col. ill. ; cm.

  The material in this book has
appeared previously in Beadstyle
Magazine.
    ISBN: 978-0-87116-286-1

1. Beadwork--Handbooks, manuals,
etc. 2. Beadwork--Patterns. 3. Jewelry
making--Handbooks, manuals, etc. I.
Title: Big and bold. II. Title: BeadStyle
Magazine.
TT860 .B54 2009
745.594/2

contents

86

36

BOLD Components 35

BIG & BOLD Effects 63

Contributors. 95

Introduction

You are a strong, powerful woman who wants strong, powerful beads to showcase her style. Luckily for you, bold looks are the key to fashion: Big jewelry is everywhere, from magazines to movies, and chunky bracelets, layers of necklaces, and eye-catching earrings are all over the runway.

It's time to create your own red-carpet look with this stunning collection of beaded necklaces, bracelets, and earrings, carefully selected from the editor-tested projects in *BeadStyle* magazine. You're sure to find the perfect necklace, bracelet, or earrings to complement any outfit.

Make fun, fashionable pieces guaranteed to attract attention with *Big & Bold*'s clear step-by-step instructions, detailed photos, and complete materials lists. Choose from projects with substantial pendants, multiple strands, or large, beautiful beads. Check out "Berries and bubbly" (p. 18) to learn how to use big beads to create a dramatic effect. Incorporate an attention-grabbing component in "String a bold pendant" (p. 52). Or see how multiple strands of beads added together create a bold overall look with the dramatic, nine-strand necklace on p. 64. All the projects are simple enough for a beginning beader but so stunning that beaders of all skill levels will want to try them.

Creating fashionable, wearable jewelry is fast and easy with the projects in *Big & Bold*. So get inspired by big beads and bold components, and make the perfect jewelry to show off your style!

Materials and tools

MATERIALS

The tools and materials you'll need for these projects are available in bead and craft stores, through catalogs, and online.

A head pin looks like a long, thick, blunt sewing pin. It has a flat or decorative head on one end to keep the beads from falling off. Head pins come in different diameters, or gauges, and lengths ranging from 1–3 in. (2.5–7.6cm).

Eye pins are just like head pins, except that they have a round loop on one end instead of a head. You can make your own eye pins from wire or head pins.

A jump ring is used to connect two loops or make chain mail. It is a small wire circle or oval that is either soldered or comes with a split that you can twist open and closed.

Split rings are used like jump rings, but they are much more secure. They look like tiny key rings and are made of springy wire.

Crimp beads are small, large-holed, thin-walled metal beads designed to be flattened or crimped into a tight roll. Use them when stringing jewelry on flexible beading wire.

Crimp ends and pinch ends are used to connect the ends of leather, suede, or other lacing materials to a clasp.

Clasps come in many sizes and shapes. Some of the most common are the toggle, the lobster claw, the magnetic, the S-hook, the box, the slide, and the hook and eye.

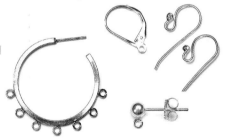

Earring wires come in a huge variety of metals and styles, including post, lever-back, French hook, and hoop. You will almost always want a loop on earring findings so you can attach beads.

Use bead caps to enclose or set off large-hole beads. Bead caps come in many different shapes and styles.

Flexible beading wire consists of fine wires that have been twisted or braided together, and it comes in a variety of sizes. Use thicker varieties (.018 or .019) when stringing heavy beads, and use thinner varieties (.014 or .015) for stringing smaller beads and pearls.

Leather or satin cord is usually used in designs in which the stringing material is featured rather than hidden.

Wire is used to make loops and eye pins or to wrap beads creatively. The smaller the gauge, the thicker the wire.

Memory wire is steel spring wire; it's used for coil bracelets, necklaces, and rings.

Chainnose pliers have smooth, flat inner jaws and tips that taper to a point so you can get into tiny spaces. Use them for gripping and for opening and closing loops and jump rings.

Crimping pliers have two grooves in their jaws to enable you to fold or roll a crimp into a compact shape.

A bench block provides a hard, smooth surface on which to hammer your pieces. An anvil is similarly hard but has different surfaces, such as a tapered horn, to help forge wire into different shapes.

Roundnose pliers have smooth, tapered, conical jaws used to form loops. The closer to the tip you work, the smaller the loop will be.

Use split-ring pliers to simplify opening split rings by inserting a curved jaw between the wires.

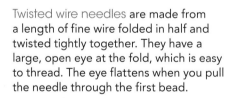

Metal files are used to refine and shape the edges of metal and wire surfaces.

Twisted wire needles are made from a length of fine wire folded in half and twisted tightly together. They have a large, open eye at the fold, which is easy to thread. The eye flattens when you pull the needle through the first bead.

On diagonal wire cutters, the outside (back) of the blades meets squarely for a flat-cut surface. The inside (front) of the blades makes a pointed cut.

Use a hammer to harden and flatten wire for strong connections. Any hammer with a flat head will work, as long as the head is free of nicks that could mar your metal. The lightweight ballpeen hammer shown here is one of the most commonly used hammers for jewelry making.

Basics

WIREWORK

Cutting flexible beading wire

Some instructions recommend a wire length to work with. If none is given (or to adjust the given length), decide how long your necklace will be, add 6 in. (15cm) (5 in./13cm for a bracelet), and cut a piece of beading wire to that length.

Cutting memory wire

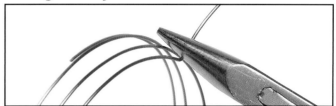

Memory wire is hardened steel, so it will dent and ruin the jaws of most wire cutters. Use heavy-duty wire cutters or cutters specifically designed for memory wire, or bend the wire back and forth until it snaps.

LOOPS AND JUMP RINGS

Plain loop

1. Trim the wire or head pin ⅜ in. (1cm) above the top bead. Make a right-angle bend close to the bead.
2. Grab the wire's tip with roundnose pliers. The tip of the wire should be flush with the pliers. Roll the wire to form a half circle. Release the wire.

3. Reposition the pliers in the loop and continue rolling.
4. The finished loop should form a centered circle above the bead.

Wrapped loop

  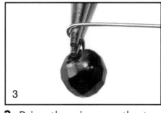 

1. Make sure you have at least 1¼ in. (3.2cm) of wire above the bead. With the tip of your chainnose pliers, grasp the wire directly above the bead. Bend the wire above the pliers into a right angle.
2. Using roundnose pliers, position the jaws in the bend.

3. Bring the wire over the top jaw of the roundnose pliers.
4. Reposition the pliers' lower jaw snugly into the loop. Curve the wire downward around the bottom of the roundnose pliers. This is the first half of a wrapped loop.

5. Position the chainnose pliers' jaws across the loop.
6. Wrap the wire tail around the wire stem, covering the stem between the loop and the top bead. Trim the excess wire, and press the cut end close to the wraps with chainnose or crimping pliers.

Opening and closing loops or jump rings

1. Hold the loop or jump ring with two pairs of chainnose pliers or chainnose and roundnose pliers, as shown.
2. To open the loop or jump ring, bring one pair of pliers toward you and push the other pair away. String materials on the open loop or jump ring. Reverse the steps to close the loop or jump ring.

CRIMPS

Flattened crimp

1. Hold the crimp using the tip of your chainnose pliers. Squeeze the pliers firmly to flatten the crimp.
2. Tug the wire to make sure the crimp has a solid grip. If the wire slides, repeat the steps with a new crimp.

Folded crimp

1. Position the crimp bead in the notch closest to the crimping pliers' handle.
2. Separate the wires and firmly squeeze the crimp.
3. Move the crimp into the notch at the pliers' tip and hold the crimp as shown. Squeeze the crimp bead, folding it in half at the indentation.
4. Test that the folded crimp is secure.

End crimp

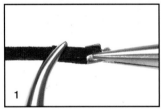

1. Glue one end of the cord and place it in a crimp end. Use chainnose pliers to fold one side of the crimp end over the cord.
2. Repeat with the second side of the crimp end and squeeze gently.

KNOTS

Overhand knot

Make a loop and pass the working end through it. Pull the ends to tighten the knot.

Surgeon's knot

Cross the right end over the left end and go through the loop. Go through again. Pull the ends to tighten. Cross the left end over the right end and go through once. Pull the ends to tighten.

Lark's head knot

Fold a cord in half and lay it behind a ring, loop, etc. with the fold pointing down. Bring the ends through the ring from back to front, then through the fold and tighten.

BIGBeads

PATTERN
Play

by Anne Nikolai Kloss

Carved beads
in muted colors
create an earthy
multistrand
necklace

Eye-catching effects in jewelry can come from grouping several ropes of beads together or by using large beads — and this necklace does both! Creating and manipulating patterns was likely a rudimentary part of your elementary school math and art classes, and you can reawaken those skills here as you create simple or complex patterns. Before stringing, lay out the long carved beads to get placement ideas. For example, do you want to separate light and dark tones, or keep them mixed? Try staggering the carved beads and alternating the two seed bead colors to create a subtle pattern and color transition.

Supply List

necklace 24 in. (61cm)
- **35–40** assorted carved horn and bone beads, 20–38mm
- **35–40** 4mm brass nuggets or 5g size 6º seed beads, metallic bronze
- **20g** size 6º seed beads, matte black
- **20g** size 6º seed beads, gold
- **140–160** 3mm brass spacers
- **10** 3mm spacer beads
- flexible beading wire, .014 or .015
- **10** crimp beads
- five-strand clasp
- chainnose or crimping pliers
- diagonal wire cutters

1 Cut five strands of flexible beading wire (Basics, p. 7). String a crimp bead, a 3mm spacer bead, and a clasp loop on each strand. Go back through the beads and crimp the crimp beads (Basics).

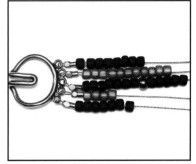

2 String a varied amount of 6º seed beads on each strand, covering the wire tails and alternating the colors on the strands.

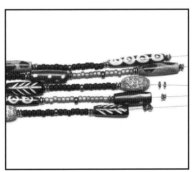

3 String two brass spacers, a carved bead, and two brass spacers on each strand.

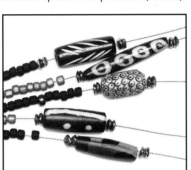

4 String seven 6ºs, a bronze seed bead or 4mm brass nugget, and seven 6ºs.

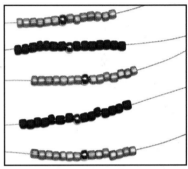

5 Repeat steps 3 and 4 until you have strung seven or eight carved beads on each strand, depending on your desired length. End by repeating step 3.

6 String 6ºs until each strand is within 1 in. (2.5cm) of the desired length. String a crimp bead, a 3mm spacer, and the respective loop on the remaining clasp half. Go back through the beads just strung plus one or two more. Tighten the wires, check the fit, and add or remove an equal number of beads on each strand if necessary. Crimp the crimp beads and trim the excess wires.

Bold and BEAUTIFUL

Dangles swing from a coiled cuff • **by Heather Powers**

A flat, multihole bead or spacer is the perfect unifying element for the coils of this bold cuff bracelet. The large polymer clay bead stabilizes the memory wire and is complemented by an eclectic mix of no fewer than six dangles. Seed beads and accent beads in several sizes and colors showcase the colors in the art bead; a different art bead might lead your color selection in a different direction.

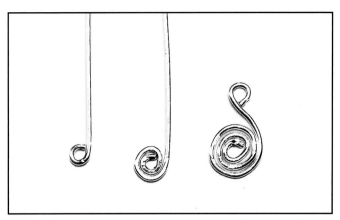

1 String a 6mm accent bead onto a head pin. Repeat with the three remaining 6mm beads, adding a 2mm spacer bead on one. String a 4mm accent bead and a flat spacer onto a head pin. Make a plain loop (Basics, p. 7) above each bead, creating five dangles. Set aside.

2 To make a wire dangle, trim the end from a head pin. Use roundnose and chainnose pliers to turn a spiral. Make a plain loop above the spiral. This will be your sixth dangle. Set aside.

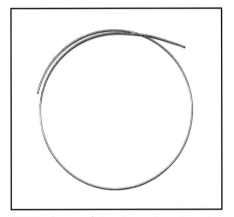

3 Use heavy-duty wire cutters to cut six 1⅓-coil pieces of memory wire (Basics). On each piece, use chainnose pliers to straighten the curve about 1 in. (2.5cm) from one end.

4 String the straightened end of a piece of memory wire through the top hole in the art bead. Repeat with each wire, stringing through each subsequent hole in the art bead.

5 On one wire, string a 2mm spacer, ½ in. (1.3cm) of mixed 8º and 11º seed beads, and a 4mm accent bead. Make a plain loop at the end of the memory wire. Open the loop (Basics) on a dangle, attach it to the memory-wire loop, and close the dangle's loop.

6 On the other end of the wire, string a 2mm spacer. String seed beads on the rest of the coil and make a plain loop at the end. Repeat steps 5 and 6 with the remaining five coils of memory wire, varying the sizes and colors of beads.

7 Trim the end from a head pin and make a loop or coil at the end. Slide the pin through the six loops on the bracelet and make a matching loop at the other end.

Supply List

bracelet 2⅜ in. (6cm) diameter
- 6-hole art bead or spacer, 1½ x ⅜ in. (3.8 x 1cm) (Heather Powers, humblebeads.com)
- **4** 6mm accent beads or crystals
- **7** 4mm accent beads or crystals
- 5g size 8º seed beads, four colors
- 3g size 11º seed beads, two colors
- **13** 2mm spacer beads
- 4mm flat spacer bead
- memory wire, bracelet diameter
- **7** 2-in. (5cm) head pins
- chainnose pliers
- roundnose pliers
- diagonal wire cutters
- heavy-duty wire cutters

Outback
WOOD BEADS

Wooden beads and hemp
are a natural match

by Jane Konkel

The wood for these beads is found on the forest floor or recycled from discarded timbers in western Australia. Because of the harshness of the environment, the beads come in random shapes and sizes. The diverse forms of these large beads stand out when strung on complementary hemp twine, and cotton beads are a perfect accent to the natural palette.

SupplyList

necklace 22 in. (56cm)
- **10** 20–70mm wooden beads
- **17–21** 12mm large-hole cotton beads (Space Trader, spacetrader.com.au)
- 6–8 ft. (1.8–2.4m) waxed hemp twine

EDITOR'S TIP
For a more colorful necklace, try colored hemp twine and multicolored cotton beads.

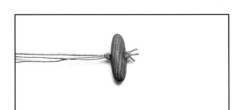

1 Decide how long you want your necklace to be. Add 7 in. (18cm) and cut three pieces of hemp twine to that length. Center three wooden beads over all three pieces.

2 On each end, over all three pieces of twine, string a cotton bead and two wooden beads.

3 On each end, over all three pieces, string two cotton beads and one wooden bead.

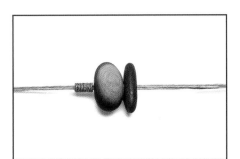

4 On each end, over all three pieces, string three to five cotton beads. Check the fit, allowing 5 in. (13cm) for finishing. Add or remove beads if necessary.

5 On each end, 3 in. (7.6cm) from the end, tie an overhand knot (Basics, p. 7) with all three pieces. On one end, string a wooden bead and tie an overhand knot. Trim the excess twine.

6 On the remaining end, string five cotton beads and tie an overhand knot on top of the existing knot. Trim the excess twine.

Wrapped
ATTENTION

Highlight a flat bead
with a wire edge

by Stacie Thompson

Paying attention to the tiniest detail can make the difference between just a nice set of earrings and something truly remarkable. A subtle metal cradle, created by wrapping a thin wire around the perimeter of a large flat bead, gives a gleam of sophistication to these bright discs. The vivid colors add some playful fun to the simplest styles.

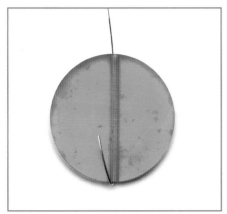

1 Cut a 12-in. (30cm) piece of wire. String a flat bead. Bend ¼ in. (6mm) of wire up at the bottom of the bead.

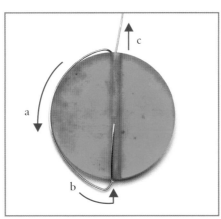

2 Wrap the long wire down and around one side of the bead **(a)** and up through the bottom hole **(b)** so the working end of the wire comes through the top of the bead **(c)**. Pull the wire taut, shaping it against the side of the bead.

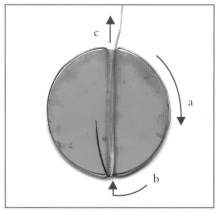

3 Repeat step 2 on the other side of the bead.

4 String three accent beads. Pulling the wire taut, make a wrapped loop (Basics, p. 7) above the top bead. Trim the ¼-in. wire hook at the bottom of the bead as close to the hole as possible.

5 Open the loop (Basics) of an earring wire. Attach the dangle and close the loop. Make a second earring to match the first.

EDITOR'S TIPS
- Make sure your flat beads have a hole that is large enough to allow the wire to pass through three times.
- Instead of cutting off the ¼-in. (6mm) wire hook in step 4, you can make a small decorative spiral.

Supply List

earrings
- 2 35mm large-hole flat beads
- 6 4–9mm accent beads in two or three shapes
- 2 ft. (61cm) 26-gauge half-hard wire
- pair of earring wires
- chainnose pliers
- roundnose pliers
- diagonal wire cutters

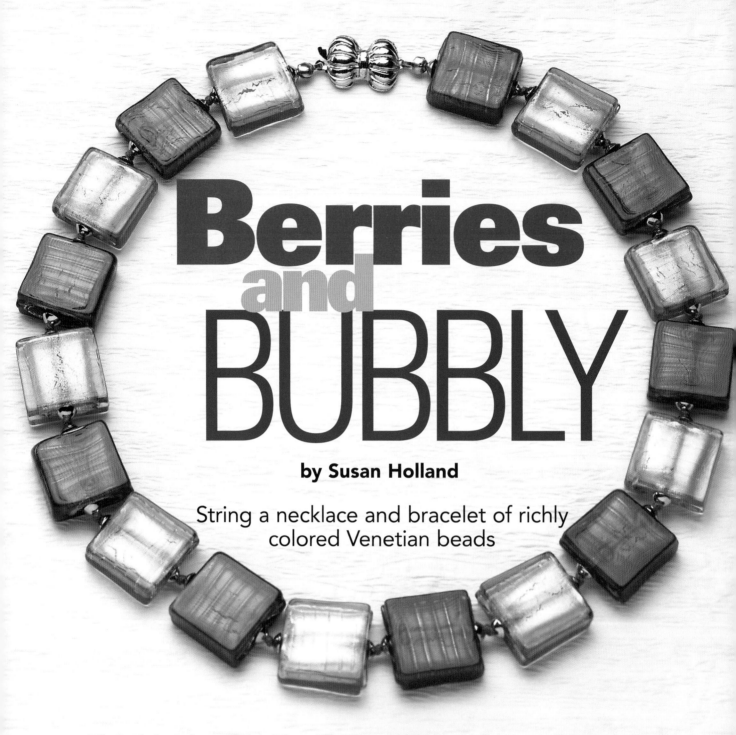

Berries
and
BUBBLY

by Susan Holland

String a necklace and bracelet of richly colored Venetian beads

The subtle colors of this Venetian glass gives this necklace a sophisticated glow. For hundreds of years, the craft of bead making has been a proud tradition in Venice; in recent years, the bead makers in Venice and Murano have wound molten glass around a copper wire to form individual beads. After allowing the beads to cool, they submerge them in acid to dissolve the wire, leaving a clean hole. This elegant necklace features large, flat square beads in Rubino Platino and Champagne Pink hues.

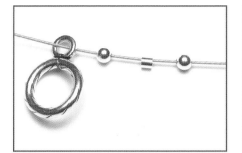

1 Cut a piece of flexible beading wire (Basics, p. 7). String a 3mm round bead, a crimp bead, a 3mm, and half of a toggle clasp.

2 Go back through the beads just strung and tighten the wire. Crimp the crimp bead (Basics) and trim the excess wire.

3 String a seed bead, a bead cap, a square bead, and a bead cap. (The open end of each bead cap should face the square.)

4 Repeat step 3, alternating raspberry- and champagne-colored squares until the necklace is within 1 in. (2.5cm) of the desired length. End with a bead cap.

5 String a seed bead, a 3mm round, a crimp bead, another 3mm, and the remaining half of the clasp.

6 Lay the necklace in a circular shape to make sure it has enough flexibility, and repeat step 2 to finish.

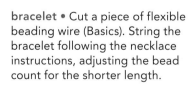

bracelet • Cut a piece of flexible beading wire (Basics). String the bracelet following the necklace instructions, adjusting the bead count for the shorter length.

Supply List

both projects
- clasp
- flexible beading wire, .018 or .019
- chainnose or crimping pliers
- diagonal wire cutters

necklace 18 in. (46cm)
- 20mm square Venetian glass beads:
  9 raspberry
  9 champagne
- **4** 3mm round silver beads
- 5g size 10º or 11º seed beads, raspberry
- **36** 5mm bead caps
- **2** crimp beads

bracelet 7 in. (18cm)
- 20mm square Venetian glass beads:
  4 raspberry
  3 champagne
- **4** 3mm round silver beads
- 1g size 10º or 11º seed beads, raspberry
- **14** 5mm bead caps
- **2** crimp beads

RAINFOREST
reinforcement

**Hand-polished
beads gleam
in a coiled
bracelet**

by Jane Konkel

Instead of wearing several
bracelets at once, get that
stacked effect by loading a
long strand of memory wire
with wooden beads and
coiling it around your wrist.
These beads come from the Zuma Beach
Bead Company and are available in a wide
variety of shapes and sizes. The beads are
hand polished and left undyed — their
warm, natural hues are strong enough on
their own.

Supply List

bracelet
- 10-bead strand of each of the following:
  - 12 x 24mm purple-heart flat oval beads
  - 10 x 17mm tempisque flat oval beads
  - 17mm rosewood round beads
  - 13mm purple-heart round beads
  - 11mm purple-heart round beads
  - 12mm purple-heart rondelles
  - 7mm rosewood cube beads
- **32–40** 3mm bicone crystals
- **14–18** 4mm spacers
- memory wire, bracelet diameter (2 in./5cm)
- **2** 2-in. (5cm) decorative head pins
- chainnose pliers
- roundnose pliers
- heavy-duty wire cutters

SUPPLY NOTE
Zuma Beach and its Central American suppliers share a commitment to sustainable resources and reforestation. Workers make wooden beads from deadfall and trimmed branches instead of cutting down trees. In an effort to replenish the rainforest and ensure a lasting supply of wood, part of the profits from the sale of these beads is used to plant new trees. To order, visit zuma-beads.com.

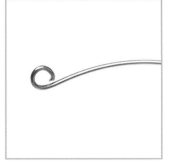

1 Separate the desired number of memory-wire coils from the stack, and add three coils. Using heavy-duty wire cutters, cut the wire (Basics, p. 7). Using roundnose pliers, make a loop at one end.

2 String a bicone crystal, a spacer, an 11mm round bead, a bicone, a 17mm round bead, a bicone, and a 13mm round bead.

3 String a bicone, a spacer, a 17mm flat oval bead, a bicone, a cube bead, a bicone, and a 24mm flat oval bead.

4 String a bicone, a spacer, a 12mm rondelle, a 17mm round, and a 12mm rondelle. Repeat step 3.

5 Repeat steps 2, 3, and 4 until the bracelet is the desired length. Check the fit, and add or remove beads if necessary. Cut the memory wire ⅜ in. (1cm) from the last bead. Make a loop on the end of the wire.

6 On a decorative head pin, string three or four beads or spacers. Make the first half of a wrapped loop (Basics). Repeat to make a second dangle.

7 Attach a dangle to each end loop and complete the wraps.

BIG BOLD

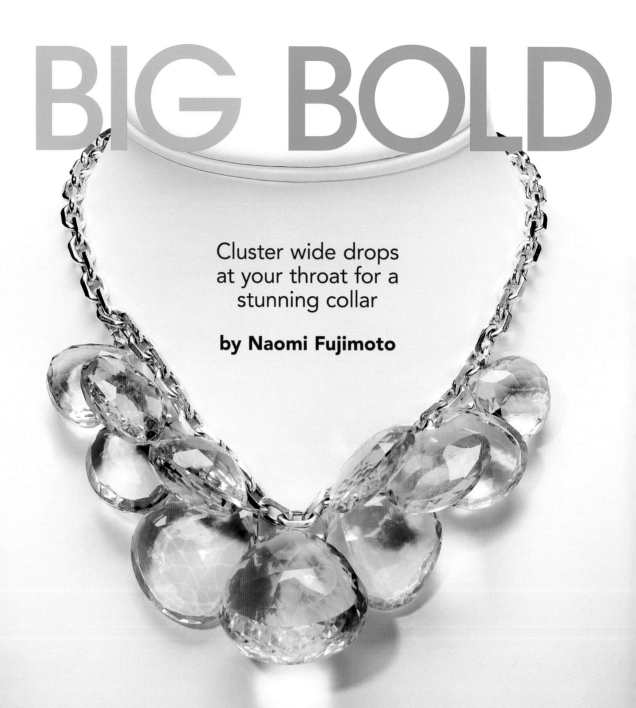

Cluster wide drops
at your throat for a
stunning collar

by Naomi Fujimoto

These briolettes are so big and bright, they
burst off of this chunky, industrial chain.
The necklace is also a breeze to make — just
string the briolettes and spacers, attach the
wire to a length of chain, and you're done!

BRIOLETTES

1 Use heavy-duty wire cutters to cut a piece of chain to the finished length.

2 Cut a 13-in. (33cm) piece of flexible beading wire (Basics, p. 7). Center the largest briolette. On each end, alternate a spacer with a briolette until you've strung all the briolettes. String a spacer, a crimp bead, and a spacer.

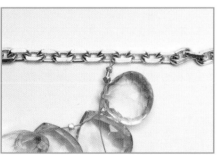

3 Center the strung briolettes and the chain. Go through the nearest chain link with each end of the beading wire. Go back through the spacers and crimp beads, and crimp the crimp beads (Basics).

4 On one end, use a jump ring (Basics) to attach a lobster claw clasp. On the other end, attach a round-bead unit.

EDITOR'S TIP
- Clustering briolettes gives your necklace an architectural feel.
- If you don't have heavy-duty wire cutters, use household pliers (rather than your jewelry pliers) to open and remove unsoldered chain links.

SUPPLY NOTE
Large (25–40mm) briolettes are typically sold by weight, strung on short strands of seven to eleven beads.

SupplyList

necklace 19 in. (48cm)
- **11–13** 25–40mm briolettes (Oriental Gemco, orientalgemco.com)
- 10mm round bead
- **14–16** 3–4mm spacers
- flexible beading wire, .018 or .019
- 17–21 in. (43–53cm) chain, 10–14mm links
- 2-in. (5cm) decorative head pin
- 7–10mm 16- or 18-gauge jump ring
- **2** crimp beads
- 20–24mm lobster claw clasp
- chainnose pliers
- crimping pliers (optional)
- roundnose pliers
- diagonal wire cutters
- heavy-duty wire cutters

DESIGN ALTERNATIVE
If you have inexpensive briolettes that don't have a consistent shape, string them in a bracelet.

A STRETCH
above the rest

Slide on a tailored, elastic bracelet

by Paulette Biedenbender

Convey a cool elegance by wearing this sleek, stretchable cuff. Moss agate is the chosen stone for this version, enhanced with silver beads. The large tiles draw attention, but the earth-toned palette keeps the bracelet classy instead of showy.

1 Measure your wrists. Double that measurement, add 5 in. (13cm), and cut two pieces of elastic to that length. Thread a beading needle on the elastic. String a rectangular bead's top holes and a round bead. Repeat until you've reached the desired length, ending with a round bead. Repeat with the second piece of elastic and the bottom hole of the rectangles.

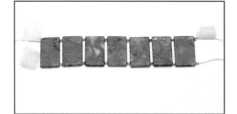

2 Check the fit, and add or remove beads as necessary. Tape three of the ends.

3 Thread the needle on the fourth strand. To connect the beads, insert the needle in the same direction through the first rectangular bead strung.

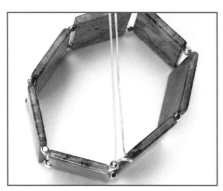

4 Continue through the remaining beads along the edge of the bracelet, exiting from the last bead strung. This will make a circular shape.

5 Remove the tape from one of the strands along the bracelet's other edge. Repeat steps 3 and 4.

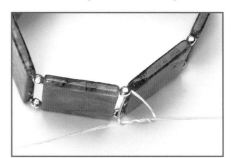

6 Remove the final piece of tape. Tie a surgeon's knot (Basics, p. 7) between a round and a rectangular bead with two adjacent strands. Dot the knot with glue and allow to dry. Trim the excess elastic. Hide the knot by pulling gently on the adjacent beads to maneuver it inside the rectangular bead. Repeat on the other edge with the remaining strands.

Supply List

bracelet
- 16-in. (41cm) strand two-holed rectangular beads, 20 x 31mm
- **14** or more 2mm round silver beads
- 3 ft. (.9m) ribbon elastic
- twisted-wire beading needle, #10
- G-S Hypo Cement
- tape
- scissors

TUBES
and
cubes

Brightly colored furnace glass earrings dance

by Karin Buckingham

Tube-shaped beads give a long, lean line to these earrings. Cube-shaped crystals and small spacers provide a visual contrast to the strong cylindrical shape of the furnace glass beads.

1 String a spacer, a cube-shaped crystal, two spacers, the furnace glass bead, and a spacer on a head pin.

2 Make a wrapped loop (Basics, p. 7) above the beads.

3 Open the loop (Basics) of an earring wire and attach the unit. Close the loop. Make a second earring to match the first.

SupplyList

earrings
- **2** 25mm (approx.) tube-shaped furnace glass beads
- **2** 4mm cube-shaped crystals
- **8** 4mm disc-shaped spacers
- **2** 3-in. (7.6cm) head pins
- pair of earring wires
- chainnose pliers
- roundnose pliers
- diagonal wire cutters

The **nature** OF THINGS

Combine slices of turquoise with coral discs and textured silver for an asymmetrical necklace and bracelet

by Arlene Schreiber

Yellow turquoise, red coral, and textured Bali silver are pronounced components on their own, but in combination, they create a striking piece of jewelry. Begin by choosing your semi-precious stones, looking for interesting and sizeable pieces. Using a larger clasp not only adds to the design but also allows you to turn a plain jump ring into a decorative finish.

1 necklace • Cut a piece of flexible beading wire (Basics, p. 7). String a clasp loop, a barrel-shaped bead, and a crimp bead. Go back through all the beads strung, tighten the wire, and crimp the crimp bead (Basics). Trim the excess wire.

2 String a coral disc, a bead cap, a 4mm bead, a 10mm Bali silver bead, a 4mm bead, and a bead cap as shown. Repeat this pattern twice.

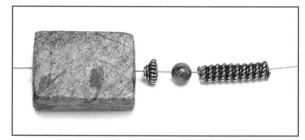

3 String a turquoise chunk, a bead cap, a 4mm bead, and a barrel-shaped bead. String the pattern in step 2 three times.

4 String a turquoise chunk, a bead cap, a 4mm bead, and a barrel-shaped bead. String the pattern in step 2 five times.

5 String a turquoise chunk, a bead cap, a 4mm bead, a bead cap, a crimp bead, a 3mm spacer bead, and a soldered jump ring. Go back through the last three beads strung, tighten the beading wire, and crimp the crimp bead. Trim the excess wire.

6 String a 3mm spacer, a 14mm coral nugget, a 6mm spacer, and a 5mm bead cap on a 2-in. (5cm) head pin.

7 Make the first half of a wrapped loop (Basic) above the end bead cap.

8 Slide the loop through the soldered jump ring the end of the necklace. Complete the wraps.

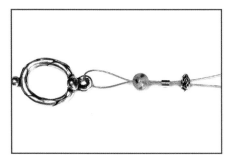

1 bracelet • Cut a piece of flexible beading wire (Basics). String half a clasp, a 4mm bead, a crimp bead, and a 4mm spacer. Go back through the beads just strung, tighten the wire, and crimp the crimp bead (Basics). Trim the excess wire.

2 String the beads as shown.

3 String a 4mm spacer, a crimp bead, a 4mm bead, and the remaining clasp half. Go back through the beads just strung, tighten the wire, and crimp the crimp bead. Trim the excess wire.

SupplyList

both projects
- flexible beading wire, .014 or .015
- chainnose and roundnose pliers
- crimping pliers (optional)
- diagonal wire cutters

necklace 17 in. (43cm)
- 16-in. (41cm) strand 4mm round turquoise beads
- **3** 18 x 22mm (approx.) rectangular yellow turquoise chunks
- 14 x 16mm (approx.) coral nugget
- **3** 6–11mm silver barrel-shaped beads
- **11** 10mm Bali silver beads
- **11** 6mm coral discs
- 3mm silver spacer
- 6mm silver spacer
- **27** 5mm bead caps
- 2-in. (5cm) head pin
- **2** crimp beads
- S-hook clasp with soldered jump rings

bracelet 8½ in. (21.6cm)
- **2** 18 x 22mm (approx.) rectangular yellow turquoise chunks
- **2** 17mm oval turquoise nuggets
- 14 x 16mm (approx.) coral nugget
- 12mm silver bead
- **2** 7mm silver beads
- 6mm coral disc
- **7** 4mm turquoise beads
- **4** 4mm silver spacers
- **2** crimp beads
- toggle clasp

Double BUBBLE

Two art-glass beads pop when strung on a solitary cord

by Lynne Dixon-Speller

Rather than display only one blown-glass art bead, double the drama by combining two shapes and letting sheer beauty speak for itself. Sometimes being bold is all about simplicity.

1 Determine the finished length of your necklace, add 3 in. (7.6cm), and cut a piece of leather cord to that length.

Center the round art bead on the cord.

2 Thread each end of the cord through the tube bead in opposite directions. Pull each end to slide the tube bead toward the round bead.

3 Check the fit and trim the leather on each end, if necessary. Attach the crimp ends (Basics, p. 7).

4 Open a jump ring (Basics) and attach it to a clasp's loop and the crimp end's loop. Close the jump ring. Repeat on the other end of the necklace, substituting a split ring for the jump ring and clasp.

SupplyList

necklace 22½ in. (57.2cm)
- blown-glass art bead, approx. 20mm round
- blown-glass art bead, approx. 14 x 27mm tube
- 2 ft. (.61m) 2mm-diameter leather cord
- 6mm split ring
- 2 crimp ends
- lobster claw clasp and jump ring
- chainnose pliers
- split-ring pliers (optional)
- G-S Hypo Cement
- scissors

Everyday

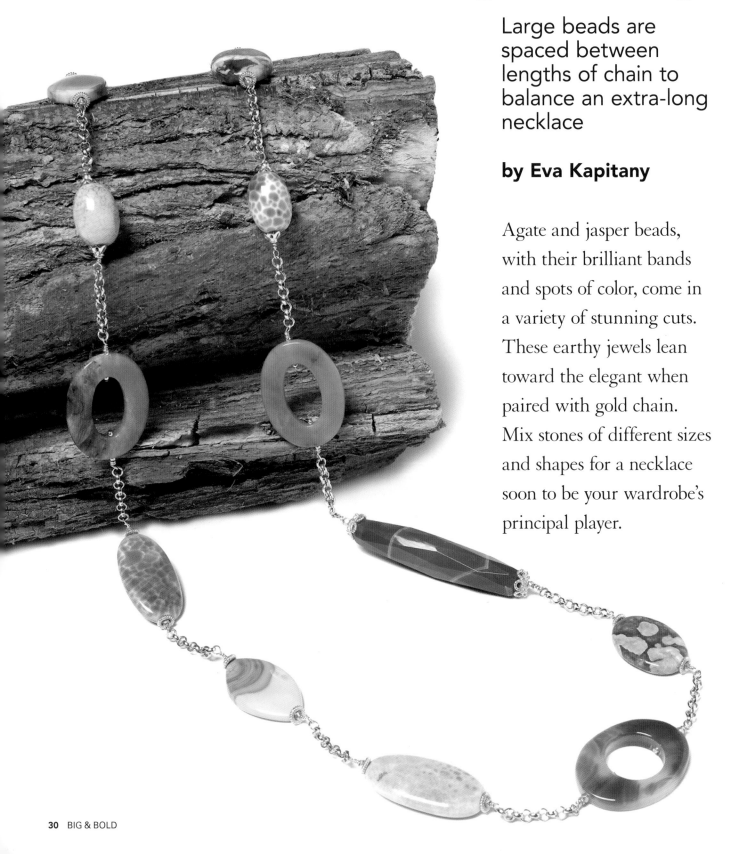

Large beads are spaced between lengths of chain to balance an extra-long necklace

by Eva Kapitany

Agate and jasper beads, with their brilliant bands and spots of color, come in a variety of stunning cuts. These earthy jewels lean toward the elegant when paired with gold chain. Mix stones of different sizes and shapes for a necklace soon to be your wardrobe's principal player.

elegance

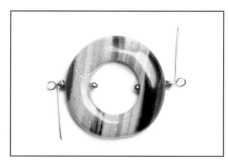

1 On a head pin, string a round spacer, an inside hole of a donut, and a faceted spacer. Make the first half of a wrapped loop (Basics, p. 7). Repeat with the donut's remaining hole. Make four donut units.

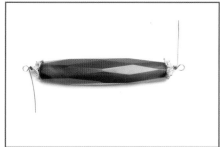

2 Cut a 4½-in. (11.4cm) piece of wire. Make the first half of a wrapped loop on one end. String: round spacer, bead cap or flat spacer, gemstone bead, bead cap or flat spacer, round spacer. Make the first half of a wrapped loop. Make six to 10 bead units.

3 Cut 10 to 14 1-in. (2.5cm) pieces of chain. Attach a loop of a donut unit and a chain and complete the wraps. Attach the remaining bead units, chains, and donut units, completing the wraps as you go. Attach the last chain to the first donut unit.

SupplyList

necklace (34–38 in./86–97cm)

- **6–10** 20–70mm gemstone beads
- **4** 30–50mm gemstone donuts, with two holes
- **6–12** 6mm flat spacers
- **12–18** 4mm faceted spacers
- **10–12** 3mm round spacers
- **6–8** 6–12mm bead caps
- **27–45** in. (69–1.1m) 24-gauge half-hard wire
- **10–14** in. (25–36cm) chain, 3–4mm links
- **8** 3-in. (7.6cm) head pins
- chainnose pliers
- roundnose pliers
- diagonal wire cutters

EDITOR'S TIP
In step 2, it's not necessary to cut a 4½-in. (11.4cm) piece of wire for every bead. For beads smaller than 35mm, 3-in. (7.6cm) pieces of wire should be adequate.

DESIGN ALTERNATIVE
Base metal chain and five beads placed just at the front of this necklace make it a less expensive (and quicker) option.

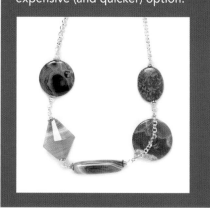

FLOWER FIELD
bracelet

by Jean Yates   Double-drilled beads
are strung together in
a great cuff

SupplyList

bracelet 6¾ in. (17.1cm)
- **5** 25mm rectangular tile beads, double drilled (Earthenwood Studio, earthenwoodstudio.com)
- **24** 4mm bicone crystals
- **24** 4mm round spacers
- flexible beading wire, .014 or .015
- **4** crimp beads
- two-strand toggle clasp
- chainnose or crimping pliers
- diagonal wire cutters

earrings
- **2** 22mm square tile beads with two loops (Earthenwood Studio)
- **22** 4mm bicone crystals
- **22** 1½-in. (3.8cm) decorative head pins
- pair of earring wires
- chainnose pliers
- roundnose pliers
- diagonal wire cutters

EDITOR'S TIP
To make your bracelet longer, string additional bicone crystals on the end of each wire until the bracelet is within 1 in. (2.5cm) of the finished length.

These double-drilled ceramic beads are available in a huge array of colors, so you control how bright or bold your jewelry will be; just determine whether you prefer a bracelet in neutral tones or cheery primary colors. The pattern of tiny jonquils led bead artist Melanie Brooks to name these "flower field" beads.

1 bracelet • Cut two pieces of flexible beading wire (Basics, p. 7). On each wire, string a bicone crystal, a spacer, the corresponding hole of a rectangular bead, a spacer, and a bicone. Repeat four times.

2 On one end of each wire, string a bicone, a spacer, a crimp bead, and the corresponding loop of half of a clasp. Repeat on the other ends of the wires. Check the fit, and add or remove beads from each end if necessary. Go back through the last few beads strung and tighten the wires. Crimp the crimp beads (Basics) and trim the excess wires.

1 earrings • On a decorative head pin, string a bicone crystal. Make the first half of a wrapped loop (Basics). Repeat to make 11 bicone units.

2 Attach the bicone unit to the loop of a square bead and complete the wraps.

3 Attach the remaining bead units, completing the wraps as you go.

4 Open the loop (Basics) of an earring wire. Attach the dangle and close the loop. Make a second earring to match the first.

BOLD
Components

CLASSIC

This green amber pendant makes a stunning focal piece, especially when accented with three complementary strands. The assortment of hues in the gemstone chips and pearls highlights the many shades of greens in the amber pendant, and assures all eyes will be on you.

trio

Showcase an amber pendant on a braided pearl-and-gemstone necklace

by Alethia Donathan

1 Cut three pieces of flexible beading wire (Basics, p. 7). Center the pendant on all three wires.

2 On each side of the pendant, over all the wires, string a 5mm bead, a 7mm bead, and a bead cap (open end facing outward).

3 Separate the strands. String 8 in. (20cm) of beads on each: on one, string a repeating pattern of 1 in. (2.5cm) of button-shaped pearls and a seed bead. String the potato-shaped pearls on another strand. String the gemstone chips on the remaining strand. Repeat on the other ends of the wires.

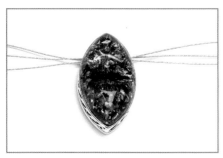

4 Braid the beaded strands loosely. Check the fit of the necklace and add or remove beads as needed.

5 On one end, over all three strands, string a 5mm bead, a spacer, a large-holed bead, the crimp, a large-holed bead, and half of a clasp. Repeat on the other side.

6 Go back through the last four beads strung. Tighten the wires and crimp the crimp bead (Basics). Trim the excess wires. Repeat on the opposite end of the necklace.

Supply List

necklace 19 in. (48cm)

- pendant (green amber; approx. 35 x 28cm)
- 16-in. (41cm) strand button-shaped pearls
- 16-in. strand potato-shaped pearls
- 36-in. (91cm) strand gemstone chips (peridot)
- 4 5mm glass beads with large holes
- 2 7mm glass beads
- 4 glass or metal beads, with holes large enough to accommodate six strands of beading wire
- 16–20 size 11º seed beads
- 2 7mm spacers
- 2 8mm bead caps
- flexible beading wire, .014 or .015
- 2 crimp beads
- clasp
- chainnose or crimping pliers
- diagonal wire cutters

GO
bohemian

by Rupa Balachandar

Jeweled earrings make for fast fashion

Big earrings are a key piece of jewelry. Go bold with filigrees decorated with brilliant crystals, including some easy-to-attach flat-back crystals. Changing the type of chain or size of crystals will create a whole new look for these free-spirited earrings.

1 Glue flat-back crystals to a filigree finding as shown, attaching nine flat backs of one color and eight of a second color. Repeat with the second finding. Allow to dry overnight.

2 On a head pin, string a 3mm bicone crystal, a 4mm bicone crystal, and a 3mm bicone. Make a plain loop (Basics, p. 7). Repeat to make nine bead units.

3 Open the loop (Basics) of a bead unit. Attach the center loop of the filigree finding. Close the loop. Attach the remaining bead units to the filigree's loops, leaving the outer loops open.

SupplyList

earrings
- **2** 50mm filigree findings with 11 loops
- **18** 4mm bicone crystals
- **36** 3mm bicone crystals
- **34** 3mm flat-back crystals, **18** in one color and **16** in a second color
- 7 in. (18cm) chain, 4–5mm links
- **18** 1-in. (2.5cm) head pins
- **6** 4–5mm jump rings
- pair of lever-back earring wires
- chainnose and roundnose pliers
- diagonal wire cutters
- Gem-Tac or Aleene's Platinum Bond Glass & Bead glue
- tweezers (optional)

4 Cut two 1½-in. (3.8cm) pieces of chain. Open a jump ring (Basics) and attach a chain to an outer loop of the filigree. Close the jump ring. Repeat to attach the second chain to the other outer loop.

EDITOR'S TIP
When gluing, hold each crystal with chainnose pliers to help you position it on a filigree finding.

5 Use a jump ring to attach both chains to an earring wire. Repeat steps 2–5 to finish the second earring.

An art bead blossoms in a silk cord necklace • **by Irina Miech**

LILY
original

Simple strands of seed beads will sprout into something spectacular when integrated with crystals, dyed silk cord, and a fabulous calla lily art bead. Because silk cords come in a multitude of intense colors, the possible combinations are endless. So your necklace, just like a lily found in nature, will be one of a kind.

1 String a bicone crystal on a head pin. Make the first half of a wrapped loop above the crystal (Basics, p. 7). Repeat to make a total of four bicone units. Set one unit aside for the extender chain in step 10.

2 a Cut a ½-in. (1.3cm) piece, a ¾-in. (1.9cm) piece, and a 1-in. (2.5cm) piece of 2mm chain. Attach a bicone unit's loop to each chain and complete the wraps.
   b Cut three 4-in. (10cm) pieces of 22-gauge wire. Make the first half of a wrapped loop on one end of each wire. Complete the wraps on two wires and set aside for step 7. On the remaining wire, attach the chain dangles and complete the wraps.

3 String a crystal rondelle, the art bead, and a rondelle on the wire. Make a wrapped loop above the rondelle.

4 Cut a piece of flexible beading wire and two pieces of silk cord to the same length. Center the pendant on the wire and silk cords.

SupplyList

necklace 15 in. (38cm)
- 60mm lily art bead pendant
- **8** 8mm crystal rondelles
- **22–26** 5mm bicone crystals
- 1g size 11º seed beads
- flexible beading wire, .014 or .015
- **2** 18–22 in. (46–56cm) silk cords, in 2 colors
- 12 in. (30cm) 22-gauge half-hard wire
- 2½ in. (6.4cm) chain, 5mm links
- 2½ in. (6.4cm) chain, 2mm links
- **4** 1½-in. (3.8cm) head pins
- **2** 24mm beading cones
- **2** crimp beads
- S-hook clasp
- chainnose pliers
- crimping pliers (optional)
- roundnose pliers
- diagonal wire cutters

EDITOR'S TIP
Depending on the size of the art bead, you may need to turn the 8mm crystal rondelle sideways in order to fit it in the top of the flower. If this is the case, string the wire through the rondelle after it is inside the art bead.

SUPPLY NOTE
The lily art bead pendants are created by Gregory Hoff. Contact him at 719-527-7668 or via e-mail at flameworkerg@gmail.com.

5 On each end of the wire, string: bicone, rondelle, bicone, 13–16 11º seed beads. Repeat this pattern twice.

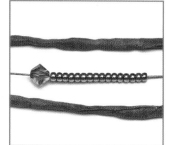

6 On each end of the wire, string a bicone and 13–16 11ºs. Repeat this pattern until the necklace is within 2 in. (5cm) of the desired length.

7 On each end of the beading wire, string a crimp bead, an 11º, and the wrapped loop of the wire from step 2b. Go back through the last three beads and tighten the wire. Check the fit, and add or remove an equal number of beads from each end if necessary. Crimp the crimp beads (Basics). String both ends of silk cord through the wrapped loop.

8 Tie the ends of the silk cord in a overhand knot. Trim the ends. On each wire end, string a beading cone and a bicone.

9 On one end, make a wrapped loop above the bicone. Attach an S-hook clasp to the loop.

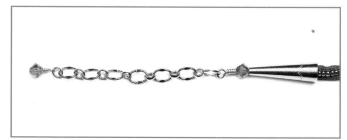

10 On the other end, make the first half of a wrapped loop above the bicone. Attach the 5mm chain and complete the wraps. Attach the bicone unit from step 1 to the end link of chain and complete the wraps.

COSMIC RINGS
bracelet

Use uncommon crystals in a distinctive bracelet-and-earrings set

by Karla Schafer

Two crystal cosmic rings stacked together make a prominent focal piece for an easy bracelet. The faceted rings create a fancy contrast to casual leather cord. Add a quick pair of earrings for a just-right balance of edgy and elegant.

1 bracelet • Cut a 10-in. (25cm) piece of leather cord. Center two cosmic rings on it. Over both ends, string two or three soldered jump rings or decorative rings.

2a With both ends, tie an overhand knot (Basics, p. 7) next to the rings.
b Repeat steps 1 and 2a, centering the new cord on the cosmic rings from step 1.

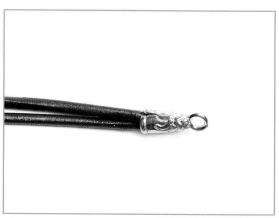

3 On each side, trim the ends to within 1 in. (2.5cm) of the finished length and apply glue. Attach a crimp end (Basics).

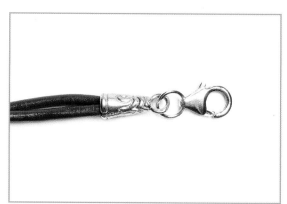

4 Open a jump ring (Basics) and attach a loop of a crimp end and a lobster claw clasp. Close the jump ring. Repeat on the other end, substituting a soldered jump ring or decorative ring for the clasp.

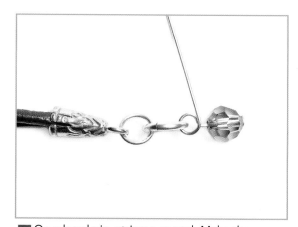

5 On a head pin, string a crystal. Make the first half of a wrapped loop (Basics). Attach the soldered jump ring or decorative ring and complete the wraps.

1 **earrings** • Open a jump ring (Basics) and attach a pendant and a soldered jump ring or decorative ring. Close the jump ring.

2 Open a jump ring and attach the soldered jump ring or decorative ring and an earring wire. Close the jump ring. Make a second earring to match the first.

EDITOR'S TIPS
• Select the 30mm crystal cosmic rings first, since there are fewer colors available in this size than in smaller sizes.
• Before placing the leather ends in a crimp end, make sure to trim both ends evenly.

DESIGN ALTERNATIVE
Feeling square? This version features square cosmic rings, square decorative rings, and a square crystal for the dangle, and substitutes four 1mm pieces of leather cord for the two 2mm pieces.

Supply List

bracelet 6 in. (15cm)
• 30mm crystal cosmic ring (Auntie's Beads, auntiesbeads.com)
• 20mm crystal cosmic ring (Auntie's Beads)
• 6mm crystal
• 16–20 in. (41–51cm) round leather cord, 2mm diameter
• 1½-in. (3.8cm) head pin
• 2 5mm jump rings
• 5–7 7mm soldered jump rings or decorative rings
• 2 crimp ends, 3mm opening
• lobster claw clasp
• chainnose pliers
• roundnose pliers
• diagonal wire cutters
• G-S Hypo Cement

earrings
• 2 20mm crystal column pendants (Auntie's Beads)
• 4 7mm jump rings
• 2 7mm soldered jump rings or decorative rings
• pair of earring wires
• chainnose pliers
• roundnose pliers
• diagonal wire cutters

Combine charms
IN MIXED-METAL EARRINGS

Parallel charm sizes create
balanced earrings

by Brenda Schweder

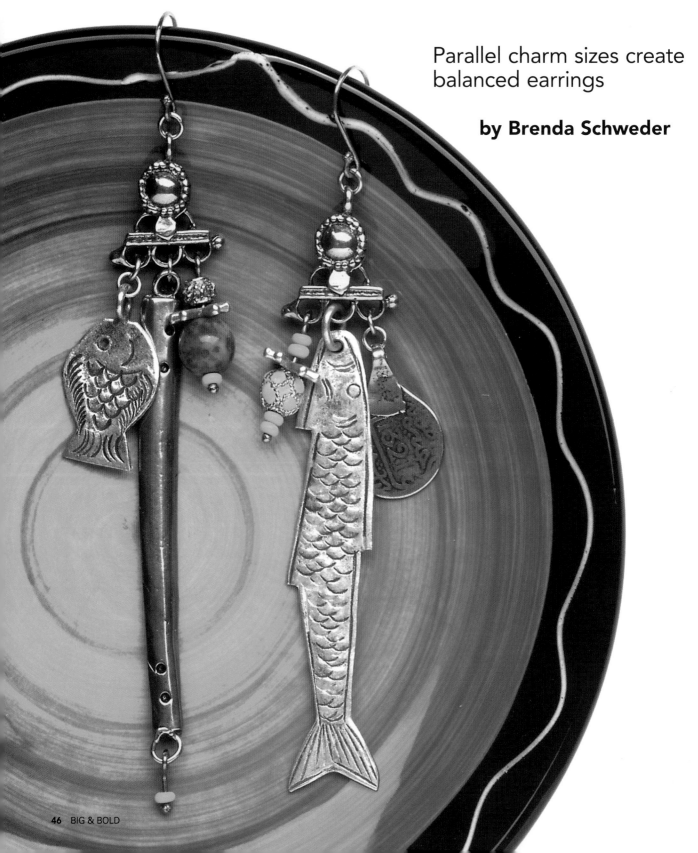

With mismatched earrings, you won't have to fish around for a fun accessory. The key to these earrings is proportion; the length of each earring balances the other. A bit of aqua adds color and keeps them bright and cheerful.

1 To make the first earring: On a decorative head pin, string a 3mm bead. Make a plain loop (Basics, p. 7). On another decorative head pin, string a 3mm bead, an 8mm bead, a flat spacer, and a 5mm spacer. Make a plain loop.

2 Open the loop of the smaller bead unit (Basics). Attach the loop of the narrow end of a tapered bar. Close the loop.

Open a 4mm jump ring (Basics). Attach the tapered bar to a connector's center loop. Close the jump ring.

3 Use two 4mm jump rings to attach a small fish charm to an outer loop of the connector. Attach the larger bead unit's loop to the remaining outer loop.

4 To make the second earring: On a decorative head pin, string two 3mm beads, a 6mm bead, a flat spacer, and two 3mm beads. Make a plain loop.

5 Use a 5–6mm jump ring to attach a large fish charm to a connector's center loop. Connect a jump ring to a coin. Use a second jump ring to attach the dangle to the outer loop of the connector. Attach the bead unit's loop to the remaining outer loop.

6 Open a 4mm jump ring and attach a dangle and the loop of an earring wire. Repeat with the other dangle.

Supply List

earrings
- 6 x 65mm tapered bar with loops
- 14 x 25mm fish charm
- 12 x 60mm fish charm
- 14mm coin with loop
- 8mm round bead
- 6mm round bead
- 6 3mm beads
- 2 8mm flat spacers
- 5mm spacer

- 2 18mm three-to-one connector bars
- 3 1½-in. (3.8cm) decorative head pins
- 5–6mm jump ring
- 7 4mm jump rings
- pair of earring wires
- chainnose pliers
- diagonal wire cutters
- roundnose pliers

Shell

GAME

Combine leather and abalone shells in an unusual necklace and bracelet

by Monica Lueder

As the focal point for this necklace, a sizeable paua shell (New Zealand abalone) donut adds a cool and iridescent gleam. The technique is simple, too. With just leather cord, abalone beads, and sterling silver jump rings — plus a few loops and dangles — you'll have this knotted collar done in no time.

1 **necklace** • String a diamond or oval shell on a 1½-in. (3.8cm) head pin and make a wrapped loop (Basics, p. 7) above the shell. Repeat nine times for a total of ten wrapped-loop dangles.

2 Cut eight 2-in. (5cm) lengths of 24-gauge wire. (Or trim the heads off of eight 2-in. head pins.) Make a plain loop (Basics) on one end of each wire. String a diamond or oval shell on six of the wires and make a plain loop above each. String a spacer on each of the two remaining wires and make a plain loop above each.

3 Tie the leather cord in a lark's head knot (Basics) around the donut.

4 String a barrel-shaped spacer over both strands and make an overhand knot (Basics) against the spacer.

5 On one strand, make an overhand knot ⅜ in. (1cm) from the center knot. String a large-hole spacer, a wrapped-loop dangle, and a spacer. Make an overhand knot against the spacer.

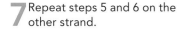

6 Make an overhand knot ⅜ in. away. String a wrapped-loop dangle and make an overhand knot against it. Repeat three times.

7 Repeat steps 5 and 6 on the other strand.

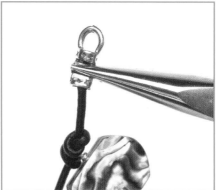

8 On each end, cut the cord ⅜ in. away from the last knot. Attach a crimp end (Basics).

9 Open a loop on a shell unit, attach it to the loop on one crimp end, and close the loop. Link the remaining loop to a soldered jump ring in the same manner.

Add a shell unit, soldered jump ring, spacer unit, soldered jump ring, shell unit, and soldered jump ring.

Repeat step 9 on the other end.

10 Check the fit. For a longer necklace, make more shell units and attach them with soldered jump rings.

On each end, open a 7mm jump ring. Attach half the clasp and close the jump ring.

bracelet 6¼ in. (15.9cm)

- abalone shell diamonds or ovals, left over from necklace
- **8** or more 6mm crystals, round or bicone
- **16** or more 3 x 5mm large-hole spacers
- **18 in.** (46cm) or more 1mm-diameter leather cord
- **16** or more 1½-in. (3.8cm) head pins
- **8** or more 6mm jump rings
- **2** 5mm jump rings or split rings
- **2** crimp ends
- toggle clasp
- chainnose pliers
- roundnose pliers
- diagonal wire cutters
- E6000 glue

1 bracelet • Make eight shell units, as in step 1 of the necklace. String a crystal on a head pin and make a wrapped loop. Make eight crystal units.

2 Open a 6mm jump ring. String a shell unit and a crystal unit and close the ring. Use jump rings to make a total of eight units.

3 Make an overhand knot ⅜ in. (1cm) away from the end of the leather cord. String a spacer, a shell and crystal unit, and a spacer. Make an overhand knot against the spacer. Repeat this sequence seven more times at ⅜-in. intervals.

4 Check the fit. If necessary, make additional shell and crystal units and string them as before. Finish each end with a crimp end as in step 8 of the necklace. Use a 5mm jump ring to attach each half of a toggle clasp to the crimp end's loop.

STRING
a bold
PENDANT

Carnelian and silver combine in a powerful necklace

by Rupa Balachandar

A shield-shaped pendant, carnelian nuggets, and dramatic silver tubes come together in a simple yet striking necklace. Not for the faint of heart, this necklace complements a fierce style. The best part is, you can make the necklace and earrings in less than half an hour for fantastic results without a heroic effort.

SupplyList

necklace 17½ in. (44.5cm)
- triangular silver pendant, approximately 60 x 70mm (Rupa B. Designs, rupab.com)
- 2 4½-in. (11.4cm) curved tube beads (Rupa B. Designs)
- 4 14–16mm faceted carnelian nuggets
- **4** 7mm round silver beads
- **10–18** 5mm round carnelian beads
- **10** 5mm round silver beads
- 5mm flat spacer
- flexible beading wire, .018 or .019
- 3 in. (7.6cm) chain for extender, 5–6mm links
- 2-in. (5cm) decorative head pin
- **2** crimp beads
- hook clasp
- chainnose pliers
- crimping pliers (optional)
- roundnose pliers
- diagonal wire cutters

earrings
- 2 10–15mm silver beads
- 2 5mm round carnelian beads
- 2 2-in. (5cm) decorative head pins
- pair of earring wires
- chainnose pliers
- roundnose pliers
- diagonal wire cutters

1 necklace • Cut a piece of flexible beading wire (Basics, p. 7). Center a pendant on the wire.

2 On each end, string a nugget, a 5mm silver bead, a nugget, and a 7mm silver bead.

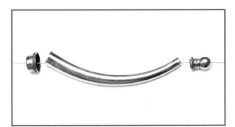

3 On each end, string the three parts of a curved tube bead.

4 On each end, string a 7mm silver bead, two carnelian beads, and two 5mm silver beads. String carnelian beads until the strand is within 2 in. (5cm) of the final length.

5 On one end, string a 5mm silver bead, a crimp bead, a 5mm silver bead, and a hook clasp. Repeat on the other end, substituting a 3-in. (7.6cm) piece of chain for the clasp. Check the fit, and add or remove beads from each end if necessary. Go back through the beads just strung and tighten the wire. Crimp the crimp beads (Basics) and trim the excess wire.

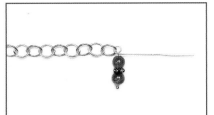

6 On a decorative head pin, string a carnelian bead, a flat spacer, and a carnelian bead. Make the first half of a wrapped loop (Basics). Attach the dangle to the end of the chain and complete the wraps.

1 earrings • On a head pin, string a carnelian bead and a silver bead. Make a wrapped loop (Basics).

2 Open the loop of an earring wire (Basics). Attach the dangle and close the loop. Make a second earring to match the first.

CLASP
distinction

A fabulous closure becomes the centerpiece for a multistrand cuff

by Linda J. Augsburg

The glisten of mirror-finished glass beads is complemented by the smoky colors of hematite and the sparkle of crystals in this five-strand bracelet. The large, multistrand clasp takes the design from simple to smashing. Like any great centerpiece, the clasp is a wonderful accent that pulls in a multitude of colors without overwhelming the delicate strands.

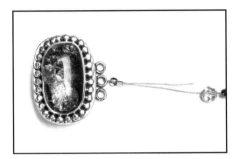

1 a Cut five strands of flexible beading wire (Basics, p. 7).
b String a crimp bead and a 3mm bead on the wire and go through the center strand of a three-strand clasp. Go back through the beads just strung, tighten the wire, and crimp the crimp bead (Basics).

2 String a crystal over the working wire and the tail. String three ovals and a crystal and repeat this pattern five or more times.

Supply List

bracelet 6¾ in. (17.1cm)
- **19** 6mm round crystals, shadow crystal
- **16-in.** (41cm) strand 3 x 5mm oval beads
- **100–120** 3mm glass beads, mirror finish
- flexible beading wire, .014 or .015
- **10** crimp beads
- 31mm three-strand box clasp
- chainnose or crimping pliers
- diagonal wire cutters

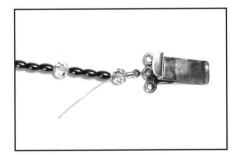

3 String a crimp bead and a 3mm bead and go through the center loop of the remaining half of the clasp. Go back through the last three beads and tighten the wire. Check the fit. (Make this bracelet snug so the clasp stays on top of your wrist.) Crimp the crimp bead and trim the excess wire.

4 Repeat step 1b, stringing through the clasp's top loop. String 3mm glass beads until the strand is the same length as the center strand. Finish as in step 3, attaching the strand to the clasp half's upper loop.

5 Repeat step 1b, again stringing through the clasp's top loop. Work above the finished strand. String two ovals, a crystal, three ovals, and a crystal, repeating the pattern five times. End with two ovals. Finish as in step 3, attaching the strand to the clasp's upper loop.

6 Repeat steps 4 and 5 through the clasp's lower loop, placing the oval and crystal strand below the 3mm strand.

Bright
as a
FEATHER

Vivid blues and greens
take flight in a bold
feather necklace

by Rupa Balachandar

Strung with turquoise, cobalt, brown, and lime-green beads, this natural pendant is the perfect accessory for your proud, brilliant self. If you're not one to strut, try a less ostentatious version with a pheasant feather.

1 Trim the feather to the desired shape and size, leaving ¼ in. (6mm) at the end of the quill. With the tip of your chainnose pliers, fold the quill's end. (If the quill fits snugly in the crimp end, trim it to ⅛ in. (3mm) and do not fold it.)

2 Insert the folded quill into a crimp end so the crimp end's loop is perpendicular to the feather. With chainnose pliers, flatten the middle section (crimp portion) of the crimp end (Basics, p. 7).

3 Cut a piece of flexible beading wire (Basics). Center the feather on the wire. String two spacers on each side.

4 On each end, string: six 4mm rounds, spacer, two rondelles, spacer, 6mm round, spacer, two rondelles, spacer.

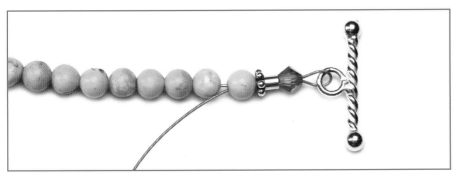

5 On each end, string 4mm rounds until the strand is within 1 in. (2.5cm) of the desired length.
On each end, string a spacer, a crimp bead, a 4mm bicone crystal, and half of the clasp. Go back through the last four beads and tighten the wires. Check the fit, and add or remove beads from each end if necessary. Crimp the crimp beads and trim the excess wire.

Supply List

necklace 16 in. (41cm)
- peacock feather
- **2** 6mm faceted round beads
- **8** 5mm rondelles
- 16-in. (41cm) strand 4mm round beads
- **2** 4mm bicone crystals
- **14** 4mm flat spacers
- flexible beading wire, .014 or .015
- **2** crimp beads
- crimp end with inner diameter to accommodate the feather's quill
- toggle clasp
- chainnose pliers
- crimping pliers (optional)
- diagonal wire cutters

LIVING
large

Look like a leading lady in a powerfully feminine necklace and earrings

by Gail Lannum

You are strong, confident, and able to see the big picture. The requisite for such a woman of substance? Substantial accoutrements. Resin and java beads accompanied by a huge silver pendant loom large, but not heavy. One tempting aspect about working with these amazonian beads is that only a few are necessary for a prominent piece. Although less is rarely more, when it comes to big beads, the truism works. So, go ahead, live large.

Supply List

pink necklace 18 in. (46cm);
green necklace 16 in. (41cm)

- large silver pendant, approx. 40–55mm (The Bead Goes On, beadgoeson.com)
- **2** 14 x 20mm silver accent beads
- **10** 14–18mm java or resin beads (green java from The Bead Goes On, pink resin from Natural Touch Beads, naturaltouchbeads.com)
- 16-in. (41cm) strand 3–5mm java or resin beads
- **12** 6-8mm flat spacers
- flexible beading wire, .024
- **2** crimp beads
- silver toggle clasp
- chainnose or crimping pliers
- diagonal wire cutters

earrings
- **2** 14 x 20mm silver accent beads
- **4** 3–5mm java or resin beads, left over from necklace
- **4** or **8** 4mm flat spacer beads
- **2** 2½-in. (6.4cm) plain or decorative head pins
- pair of earring wires
- chainnose pliers
- roundnose pliers
- diagonal wire cutters

1 necklace • Cut a piece of flexible beading wire (Basics. p. 7). Center the pendant on the wire and string 3–5mm beads on each side until they extend beyond the edges of the pendant.

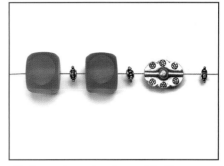

2 On each end, string a 14–18mm bead, spacer, 14–18mm bead, spacer, accent, and a spacer.

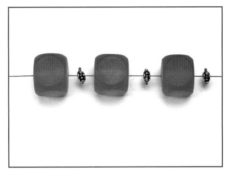

3 On each end, string an alternating pattern of three 14–18mm beads and three spacers. String 3–5mm beads on each end until the strand is within 1 in. (2.5cm) of the desired length.

4 On each end, string a crimp bead, 3–5mm bead, and half a clasp. Go back through the beads just strung and tighten the wire. Check the fit, and add or remove beads from each end if necessary. Crimp the crimp beads (Basics) and trim the excess wire.

1 earrings • String a spacer (optional) 3–5mm bead, spacer, accent, spacer, 3–5mm bead, and a spacer (optional) on a plain or decorative head pin. Make a wrapped loop (Basics) above the top bead.

2 Open the loop of an earring wire (Basics) and attach the dangle. Close the loop. Make a second earring to match the first.

SEED BEAD

Multiple strands of
seed beads take shape
in an elegant necklace

by Susan Tobias

SupplyList

necklace 19½ in. (49.5cm)
• 50 x 10mm or larger Bali silver
  curved tube
• **4** 12mm bicone crystals
• hank of size 11º seed beads
• **14** 9mm large-hole bead caps
• flexible beading wire, .014 or .015
• **9** 3mm crimp beads
• toggle clasp
• chainnose or mighty crimping
  pliers
• diagonal wire cutters

1 Cut six pieces of flexible beading wire (Basics, p. 7). Center one 3mm crimp bead on all six wires. Crimp the crimp bead (Basics). Center the Bali silver tube over the crimp. On each side, over all six wires, string a 12mm bicone crystal and a crimp bead. Crimp the crimp beads.

2 On each side, over all six wires, string two bead caps so the narrow ends meet.

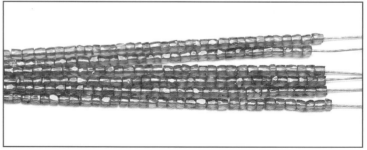

3 On each side, on each wire, string approximately 3 in. (7.6cm) of 11º seed beads.

beauty

Six seed bead strands drape between sterling silver cones in this dramatic necklace. Because the availability of large bicone crystals may be limited, choose your crystals first, then opt for matching hex-cut seed beads. A Bali-silver tube and oversized bead caps complement this dynamic piece, giving it silver shimmer.

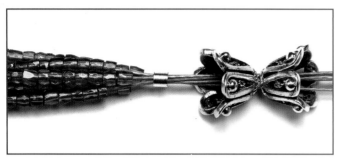

4 On each side, over all six wires, string a crimp bead and crimp it. Repeat steps 2 and 3. Check the fit, allowing 3 in. (7.6cm) for finishing. Add or remove beads if necessary. String a crimp bead, crimp it, and repeat step 2 again.

5 On each side, over all six wires, string a bicone, a crimp bead, a bead cap, and half of a clasp. Go back through the beads just strung and tighten the wires. Crimp the crimp beads, and trim the excess wire.

EDITOR'S TIP
Rather than stringing tiny seed beads individually, transfer them directly from the hank onto your beading wire. String your beading wire through the seed beads while they are still strung on the hank. Then pull the hank string out.

BIG & BOLD Effects

Prepare a feast of pearls with a multistrand necklace and drop earrings

by Teri Bienvenue

A NINE-STRAND NECKLACE IS A
bead banquet

When served together, a multitude of pearls, faceted rondelles, and seed beads is a savory complement to an engraved pendant. And for dessert, a pair of sweet earrings.

1 **necklace** • On a 1½-in. (3.8cm) decorative head pin, string a color A rondelle. Make the first half of a wrapped loop (Basics, p. 7). Repeat, making 24–30 color A rondelle units. Complete the wraps on half of the units, setting them aside for step 6.

2 Cut a 1½-in. (3.8cm) piece of chain. String two or three units on each link and complete the wraps.

3 To make a bail: Cut a 2-in. (5cm) piece of flexible beading wire (Basics). String a pendant, approximately 1¼ in. (3.2cm) of 11º seed beads, and a crimp bead. Go back through the 11ºs on each side of the crimp bead. Crimp the crimp bead (Basics) and trim the excess wire.

4 On a 2-in. (5cm) head pin, string a color A rondelle and the pendant. Make the first half of a wrapped loop, attach the chain, and complete the wraps.
   Cut eight pieces of flexible beading wire (Basics). Cut another piece 4 in. (10cm) longer. (The longest strand of this necklace is 19 in./48cm.)

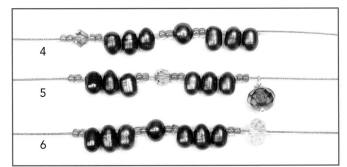

5 On the first wire, string: two 11°s, color B rondelle, two 11°s, three top-drilled pearls, two 11°s, potato-shaped pearl, two 11°s, three top-drilled pearls.

On the second wire, string: two 11°s, three top-drilled pearls, two 11°s, 6mm round crystal, two 11°s, three top-drilled pearls, two 11°s, bicone crystal.

On the longest (third) wire, center the pendant.

On each end of the longest wire, string: two 11°s, three top-drilled pearls, two 11°s, round pearl, two 11°s, three top-drilled pearls, two 11°s, bicone, 11°.

Repeat each pattern on the respective wire until each strand is within 2 in. (5cm) of the desired length.

6 On the fourth wire, string: two 11°s, bicone, two 11°s, three top-drilled pearls, two 11°s, round pearl, two 11°s, three top-drilled pearls.

On the fifth wire, string: two 11°s, three top-drilled pearls, two 11°s, 4mm round crystal, two 11°s, three top-drilled pearls, two 11°s, rondelle unit.

On the sixth wire, string: two 11°s, three top-drilled pearls, two 11°s, round pearl, two 11°s, three top-drilled pearls, two 11°s, color C rondelle.

Repeat each pattern on the respective wire until each strand is within 2 in. (5cm) of the desired length.

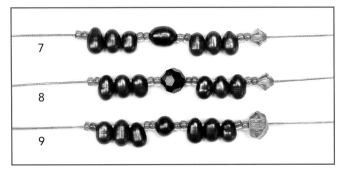

7 On the seventh wire, string: two 11°s, three top-drilled pearls, two 11°s, potato pearl, two 11°s, three top-drilled pearls, two 11°s, bicone.

On the eighth wire, string: two 11°s, three top-drilled pearls, two 11°s, 6mm round, two 11°s, three top-drilled pearls, two 11°s, bicone.

On the ninth wire, string: two 11°s, three top-drilled pearls, two 11°s, round pearl, two 11°s, three top-drilled pearls, two 11°s, color D rondelle.

Repeat each pattern on the respective wire until each strand is within 2 in. (5cm) of the desired length.

8 On each end of the first three wires, string three 11°s, a crimp bead, and a spacer. String the wires through the bottom loop of half of a box clasp. Check the fit, and add or remove beads if necessary. Go back through the beads just strung and tighten the wires. Crimp the crimp beads and trim the excess wire.

Repeat, stringing the fourth, fifth, and sixth wires through the middle loop of the box clasp and the remaining wires through the top loop of the box clasp.

SupplyList

necklace 19 in. (48cm)
- 45 x 54mm teardrop pendant with 14mm hole (Lillypilly Designs, lillypillydesigns.com)
- 16-in. (41cm) strand 6mm potato-shaped pearls
- 5 16-in. (41cm) strands 4–5mm pearls, top drilled
- 16-in. (41cm) strand 4mm round pearls

- 4 16-in. (41cm) strands 6mm faceted rondelles, in four colors
- 18–26 6mm round crystals
- 10–14 4mm round crystals
- 46–66 4mm bicone crystals
- 24g size 11° seed beads
- 18 3mm spacers
- flexible beading wire, .014 or .015
- 1½ in. (3.8cm) chain, 4–5mm links
- 2-in. (5cm) head pin

- 24–30 1½-in. (3.8cm) decorative head pins
- 19 crimp beads
- three-strand box clasp
- chainnose pliers
- crimping pliers (optional)
- roundnose pliers
- diagonal wire cutters

earrings
- 2 23 x 26mm teardrop pendants (Lillypilly Designs)

- 2 6mm potato-shaped pearls
- 2 6mm faceted rondelles
- 2 4mm spacers
- 4 in. (10cm) 24-gauge half-hard wire
- pair of earring wires
- chainnose pliers
- roundnose pliers
- diagonal wire cutters

1 earrings • Cut a 2-in. (5cm) piece of wire. Make the first half of a wrapped loop (Basics), and string a pendant. Complete the wraps.

2 String a rondelle, a spacer, and a potato-shaped pearl. Make a wrapped loop.

3 Open the loop (Basics) of an earring wire and attach the dangle. Close the loop. Make a second earring to match the first.

COILED
collar

Challenge yourself to form this elaborate collar

by Louise Jeremich

Looking for a challenging project? This necklace may be just the ticket. For a knockout effect, form three coil designs using heavy-gauge wire. Position the hammered coils in a mirrored pattern and join them with thinner wire.

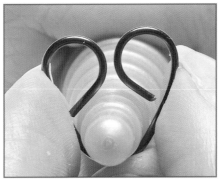

1 To make a heart coil: Cut two 3-in. (7.6cm) pieces of 16-gauge wire. Pair the wires. Wrap one end of the pair around the round tip of a mandrel or other cylindrical object to make a loop. Repeat on the other end.

Center the pair on the mandrel, and pull the loops together to form a heart shape. Use roundnose pliers to tighten each loop's center. Make two heart coils.

2 To make a type A coil: Cut two 5¼-in. (13.3cm) pieces of 16-gauge wire. Pair the wires. Wrap one end of the pair around the mandrel's tip. Make two successively larger wraps by using larger tiers of the mandrel. Flatten the coils. Repeat on the remaining end, wrapping the wire in the opposite direction. Use roundnose pliers to tighten each coil's center. Make four type A coils.

3 To make a type B coil: Cut two 6-in. (15cm) pieces of 16-gauge wire. Pair the wires. Wrap the ends of the pair as in step 2. If desired, make the bottom coil larger than the top coil. Make two type B coils.

4 To make a clasp: Cut a 4-in. (10cm) piece of 16-gauge wire. On each end, use roundnose pliers to make a small loop. Place one end on the mandrel and pull the wire around. Repeat on the remaining end in the opposite direction.

5 Cut a 2-in. (5cm) piece of 16-gauge wire. On each end, make a small loop. Center the wire on the mandrel. Pull the loop ends toward each other until they overlap.

On a bench block or anvil, hammer one half of the clasp. Turn the piece over and hammer the other side. Repeat with the remaining half of the clasp and each coil.

Supply List

necklace 21 in. (53cm)
- **10–12** 6–8mm beads
- 4 ft. (1.2m) 16-gauge copper wire or Artistic Wire
- 25–30 in. (64–76cm) 24-gauge copper wire or Artistic Wire
- 5 ft. (1.5m) 26-gauge copper wire or Artistic Wire
- 14–18 in. (36–46cm) chain, 3–4mm links
- chainnose pliers
- roundnose pliers
- diagonal wire cutters
- heavy-duty wire cutters
- bench block or anvil
- hammer
- mandrel or other cylindrical object

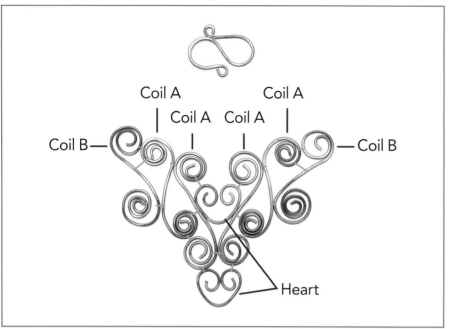

Coil A   Coil A

Coil A   Coil A

Coil B —   — Coil B

Heart

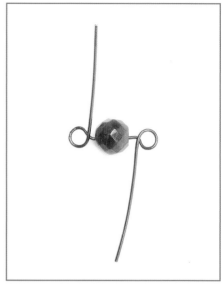

6 To attach the coils: Cut 19 3-in. (7.6cm) pieces of 26-gauge wire. Wrap one piece tightly around the hook clasp as shown. Trim the excess wire. Use chainnose pliers to tuck in the ends.

Attach the remaining coils as shown. Hammer the entire centerpiece.

7 To make a chain-and-bead section: Cut a 2½-in. (6.4cm) piece of 24-gauge wire. Make the first half of a wrapped loop (Basics, p. 7) on one end. String a bead and make the first half of a wrapped loop. Make 10–12 bead units.

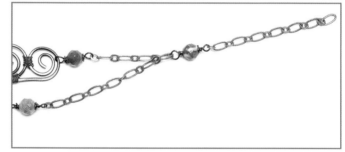

8 Cut two 1-in. (2.5cm) and six to eight 2-in. (5cm) pieces of chain. On each side, attach a bead unit's loop to the top coil of the B-coil. Attach the remaining loop to a 1-in. (2.5cm) chain. Complete the wraps as you go.

Attach a bead unit's loop to the large bottom coil of the B-coil. Attach the remaining loop to a 2-in. (5cm) chain.

9 On each side, attach one loop of a bead unit to both chains. Attach the remaining loop to a 2-in. (5cm) chain. Attach a bead unit, chain, and a bead unit. Leave the end loop unwrapped.

10 Check the fit. If necessary, trim chain or attach a chain or bead unit on each end. On each end, attach half of the clasp.

EDITOR'S TIP
Whether you form coils with a mandrel, a pen barrel, or roundnose pliers, work with two wires at once. This will help you make symmetrical coils.

Big bangle THEORY

Gumball-sized pearls star in a fabulous bracelet and earrings

by Brenda Schweder

Ah, the bangled web we weave. Try to simplify and still make an impact by wearing one striking bangle. Here, round beads, square wire, and sterling loops come together to form a single stellar bracelet. And the fun earrings, hardly an ensemble's afterthought, balance asymmetrical pearl dangles. Now your jewelry — if not your life — can be in perfect alignment.

Supply List

bracelet
- **14** 12 or 14mm round pearls
- **2** 3-in. (7.6cm) bangle bracelets with ruffled loop edges (Nina Designs, ninadesigns.com)
- 15–18 in. (38–46cm) 22-gauge half-hard square wire, sterling silver
- chainnose pliers
- roundnose pliers
- diagonal wire cutters

earrings
- **2** 12 or 14mm round pearls
- 11 in. (28cm) 22-gauge half-hard square wire, sterling silver
- pair of lever-back earring wires
- chainnose pliers
- roundnose pliers
- diagonal wire cutters

1 **bracelet** • If you're using 12mm pearls, cut 14 pieces of 1¹⁄₁₆-in. (2.7cm) wire. For 14mm pearls, cut 14 pieces of 1¼-in. (3.2cm) wire. Make a plain loop (Basics, p. 7) at one end of each piece. Make each loop large enough so that it won't slip through the bangle's loops.

2 On one wire, string a loop on the first bangle, a pearl, and a loop on the second bangle.

3 Bend the wire to form a right angle against the second bangle's loop. Make a plain loop.

4 Repeat with the other wires, attaching pearls to every fourth loop on each bangle.

DESIGN GUIDELINES

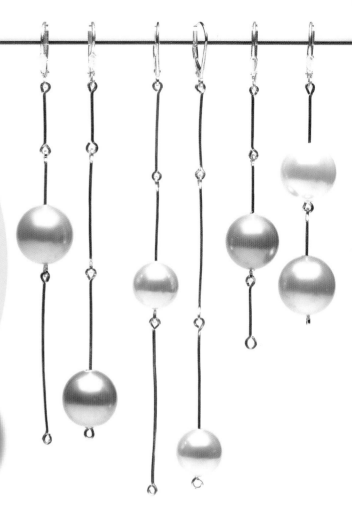

- Synthetic pearls tend to have larger holes than natural pearls. Avoid beads with small holes; fine wire will not provide enough structure for the bracelet.

- Try a monochromatic bracelet or use a pearl strand in assorted colors.

- The larger the pearl, the smaller the bracelet's inner diameter will become. Use smaller beads or coin-shaped pearls to accommodate your wrist size.

- For the bracelet and earrings, make 4mm or larger plain loops to accentuate the round design elements and leave ample room for the wire pieces to move.

- Create a pair of mismatched earrings with different colored pearls. Or make one earring with two pearls and one with a single pearl.

- When attaching each pearl to the bracelet, bend the wire into a right angle as close as possible to the bangle's frame. This will ensure a secure fit between the two bangles.

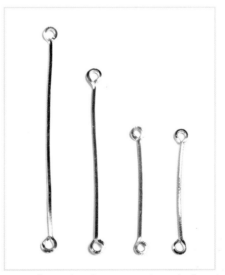

1 earrings • **a** Cut six pieces of wire, two to each of the following lengths: 1¼-in., 1¾-in., and 2¼-in. (3.2cm, 4.4cm, and 5.7cm, respectively).

b Make a plain loop (Basics) at one end of a 2¼-in. piece of wire. String a pearl and make a plain loop at the other end. Make a plain loop at one end of a 1¾-in. (4.4cm) piece of wire. String a pearl and make a plain loop at the other end.

2 Make a plain loop at each end of the four remaining pieces of wire.

3 Open the loops (Basics) on each 1¾-in. wire. Attach each to a short and a long wire, as shown. Close the loops. Open the loops on two earring wires and attach each dangle. Close the loops.

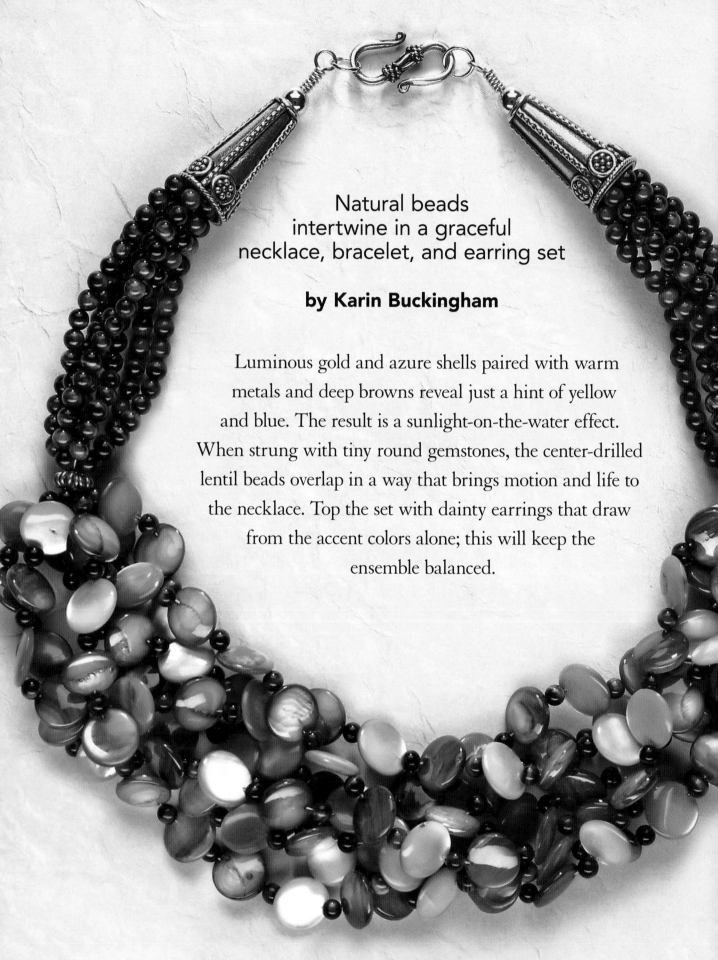

Natural beads
intertwine in a graceful
necklace, bracelet, and earring set

by Karin Buckingham

Luminous gold and azure shells paired with warm
metals and deep browns reveal just a hint of yellow
and blue. The result is a sunlight-on-the-water effect.
When strung with tiny round gemstones, the center-drilled
lentil beads overlap in a way that brings motion and life to
the necklace. Top the set with dainty earrings that draw
from the accent colors alone; this will keep the
ensemble balanced.

SHELL harmony

1 **necklace** • Cut seven pieces of flexible beading wire (Basics, p. 7). String a gemstone, a light lentil, a gemstone, and a dark lentil. Repeat until the beaded strand is 8½ in. (21.6cm) long, ending with a gemstone. Repeat on the other strands, beginning some with light lentils and some with dark lentils.

2 On each end, string a spacer over all seven wires.

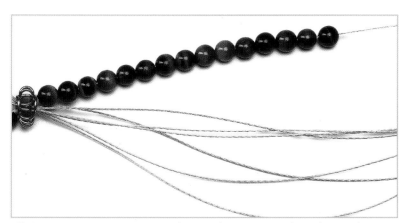

3 String 15 gemstones on each strand. Repeat on the other end. Check the fit, allowing approximately 3 in. (7.6cm) for finishing. Add or remove gemstones, if necessary.

4 Cut a 3-in. piece of 20-gauge wire. Make a wrapped loop (Basics) at one end.

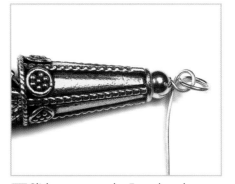

5 String a seed bead, a crimp bead, a seed bead, and the wire loop. Go back through the beads just strung. Repeat with each strand.

6 Repeat steps 4 and 5 on the other end. Tighten the wires and crimp the crimp beads (Basics). Trim the excess wire.

7 Slide a cone and a 5mm bead on the wire. Make the first half of a wrapped loop above the bead, and slide a jump ring on the loop.

8 Complete the wraps. Repeat steps 7 and 8 on the other end. Attach the clasp to one jump ring.

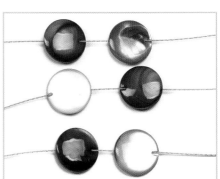

1 bracelet • Determine the finished length of your bracelet, add 5 in. (13cm), and cut three pieces of beading wire to that length (Basics). String lentils, alternating colors, until the beaded portion of each strand is within 1 in. (2.5cm) of the desired length.

2 String two seed beads, a crimp bead, two seed beads, and the corresponding loop on half the clasp. Go back through the beads just strung. Repeat on the other end. Tighten the wires, check the fit, and add or remove beads, if necessary. Crimp the crimp beads (Basics) and trim the excess wire.

SupplyList

necklace 18 in. (46cm)
- **2** 15-in. (38cm) strands 11–12mm lentils (Fire Mountain Gems, firemountaingems.com)
- **2** 16-in. (41cm) strands 11–12mm lentils (Fire Mountain Gems)
- **4** 16-in. strands 4mm round gemstones
- **2** 5mm round beads
- **1g** size 11º seed beads
- **2** 7mm large-hole spacer discs
- flexible beading wire, .014 or .015
- **6 in.** (15cm) 20-gauge wire
- **2** soldered jump rings
- **2** 12 x 25mm cones
- **14** crimp beads
- S-hook clasp
- chainnose pliers
- crimping pliers (optional)
- roundnose pliers
- diagonal wire cutters

bracelet 8 in. (20cm)
- 11mm–12mm lentils, left over from necklace
- size 11º seed beads, left over from necklace
- flexible beading wire, .014 or .015
- **6** crimp beads
- three-strand clasp
- chainnose or crimping pliers
- diagonal wire cutters

earrings
- **6** 4mm round gemstones
- **10** 3mm round beads
- **8** 2-in. (5cm) head pins
- **2** 7 x 10mm cones
- pair of earring wires
- chainnose pliers
- roundnose pliers
- diagonal wire cutters

1 **earrings •** String a gemstone and a 3mm round on a head pin. Make a plain loop (Basics) above the top bead. Make a total of three bead units.

2 Trim the head from a head pin and make a plain loop at the end. Open the loop (Basics), attach the gemstone dangles, and close the loop.

3 String a 3mm bead, a cone, and a 3mm bead on the head pin.

4 Make a wrapped loop (Basics) above the top bead. Open the loop of an earring wire and attach the dangle. Close the loop. Make a second earring to match the first.

CHRYSOPRASE
cuff

A coiled strand of chrysoprase makes a cheery bracelet

by Naomi Fujimoto

Pair gemstone nuggets with sunny gold and yellow tones like olive or lemon jade. The multitude of beads makes this cuff instantly noticeable, and bright green and yellow are lush color choices.

1 bracelet • Using heavy-duty wire cutters, cut a piece of memory wire about six coils long (Basics, p. 7). Use roundnose pliers to make a loop on one end.

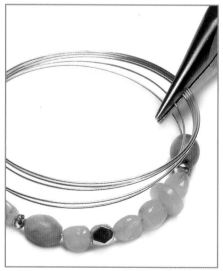

2 String nuggets, interspersing accent beads and faceted rondelles, until the bracelet is the finished length.

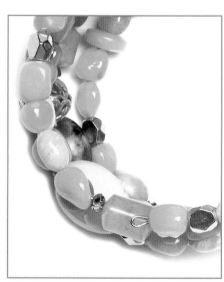

3 Make a loop and trim the excess wire.

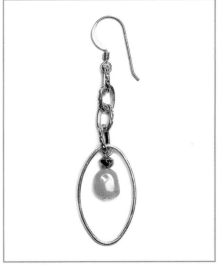

1 earrings • On a head pin, string a nugget and a faceted rondelle. Make a plain loop (Basics).

2 Cut a 2-in. (5cm) piece of chain. Open the bead unit's loop and attach a small link as shown. Close the loop.

3 Open the loop of an earring wire (Basics). Attach the dangle and close the loop. Make a second earring to match the first.

DESIGN ALTERNATIVE
Try gold-plated Czech glass beads instead of faceted rondelles, available from Eclectica (262-641-0910).

Make super-long earrings with cascading pearls and crystals

by Camilla Jorgensen

If you're keeping a low profile, you might want to leave these earrings at home. You'll surely get a shower of attention sporting these gleaming torrents of beads. Make a few pairs — varying the length and the materials — and your look can change like the weather.

RAINING style

1 **a** Cut an 18-in. (46cm) piece of Fireline. String a pearl about 1 in. (2.5cm) from one end and position it on your index finger.

b Wrap the working end of the line around your finger and to the left of the pearl to form a loop.

2 Slide the loop off of your finger, and string the working end of the line through the loop from front to back.

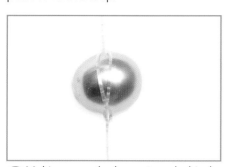

3 Making sure the loop stays behind the pearl, hold the pearl while tightening the knot.

4 Apply a dot of glue in the hole nearest the knot and string the tail back through the hole, pulling it tight. Trim the tail.

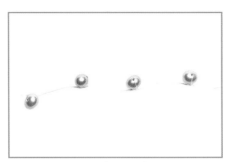

5 Repeat steps 1b to 3, knotting a pearl every ½ in. (1.3cm), until the beaded strand is within 1 in. (2.5cm) of the finished length. Make a total of five pearl-only strands and four strands alternating pearls and 5mm bicone crystals.

6 String the strands through a bead tip and tie an overhand knot (Basics, p. 7) about ½ in. from the top pearls. Apply glue to the knot and trim the excess line. Use chainnose pliers to close the bead tip over the knot.

7 Open the loop (Basics) of the bead tip. Attach the dangle to the loop of an earring wire. Close the loop. Make a second earring to match the first.

Supply List

earrings
- 40–48 5mm bicone crystals
- 2 16-in. (41cm) strands 4mm potato pearls
- Fireline 6 lb. test
- 2 clamshell bead tips
- pair of earring wires
- chainnose pliers
- roundnose pliers
- E6000 adhesive

DESIGN ALTERNATIVE
Create smoky earrings with shorter strands, darker beads, and beading thread.

EDITOR'S TIP
Thicker stringing material, such as monofilament, will give the earrings a more sculptural look.

Substantial
Style
with a twist

Multiple gemstone and pearl
strands create a lush look

by Juliana Thaens

Combine seven strands of gemstones and pearls for an eye-catching necklace that is bound to be noticed. Twist the necklace before you put it on, and it will gleam with luster and color. Keep the earrings simple so they don't compete with the necklace; lentil drops do the trick.

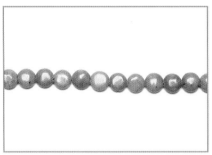

1 necklace • Cut seven pieces of flexible beading wire (Basics, p. 7). On one wire, string lentil beads until the strand is within 1 in. (2.5cm) of the finished length.

2 On the remaining wires, string gemstones or pearls until the strands are within 1 in. (2.5cm) of the finished length. Set aside two pearls for step 7.

3 On each end of three wires, string a spacer. Over all three wires, string a crimp bead and a soldered jump ring or split ring.

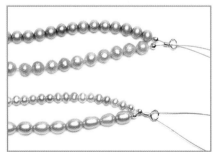

4 On each end of two wires, string a spacer. Over both wires, string a crimp bead and a soldered jump ring. Repeat with the two remaining wires.

Supply List

necklace 16 in. (41cm)
- 16-in. (41cm) strand 8–10mm gemstone lentil beads
- 16-in. (41cm) strand 4–6mm gemstone beads
- **5** 16-in. (41cm) strands 3–7mm pearls, assorted shapes
- **15** 3–4mm round spacers
- flexible beading wire, .014 or .015
- 2 in. (5cm) chain for extender, 5–7mm links
- 2-in. (5cm) head pin
- **2** 8–10mm jump rings
- **6** 5–6mm soldered jump rings or split rings
- **6** 2mm crimp beads
- 18–20mm lobster claw clasp
- chainnose pliers
- crimping pliers
- roundnose pliers
- diagonal wire cutters

earrings
- **2** 8–10mm gemstone lentil beads
- **2** 1½-in. (3.8cm) decorative head pins
- **2** 5–6mm soldered jump rings
- pair of earring wires
- chainnose pliers
- roundnose pliers
- diagonal wire cutters

5 Check the fit of all seven strands, and add or remove beads if necessary. Go back through the beads just strung and tighten the wires. Make folded crimps (Basics) and trim the excess wire.

6 Open a large jump ring (Basics) and attach the three soldered jump rings and a lobster claw clasp on one side. Close the jump ring. Repeat on the other side, substituting a 2-in. (5cm) piece of chain for the clasp.

7 On a head pin, string a spacer and two pearls. Make the first half of a wrapped loop (Basics). Attach the bead unit to the chain and complete the wraps.

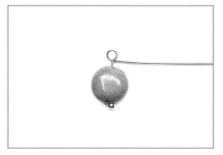

1 earrings • On a decorative head pin, string a lentil bead and make the first half of a wrapped loop (Basics).

2 Attach the bead unit to a soldered jump ring and complete the wraps.

3 Open the loop (Basics) of an earring wire. Attach the dangle and close the loop. Make a second earring to match the first.

DESIGN ALTERNATIVE
To add sparkle, incorporate faceted glass and crystal into the strands.

EDITOR'S TIP
If you want your necklace to be significantly longer than 16 in. (41cm), double the number of gemstone and pearl strands you buy. If you want to add only a little length, string two to four extra beads on each end of the strands. As long as the extra beads match the general color scheme, they don't need to be an exact match.

TWISTED cuffs

Use wire to big effect

by Wendy Witchner

by Wendy Witchner

These substantial silver bracelets may not look like beginner projects, but they're easy to do and simple to modify. Choose a favorite shape or pattern that complements your wardrobe for the broad geometric centerpiece. Or if you're looking for a project to make for the man in your life, leave out the central design to give the cuff unisex appeal.

SupplyList

all cuffs
- chainnose pliers
- roundnose pliers
- diagonal wire cutters
- ball-peen hammer
- bench block or anvil
- metal file or emery board

cuff with large spiral or triangle
- 2 ft. (61cm) 14-gauge sterling silver wire
- 5 ft. (1.5m) 22-gauge twisted sterling silver wire

cuff with small spiral
- 1 ft. (30cm) 14-gauge sterling silver wire
- 5 ft. 22-gauge twisted sterling silver wire

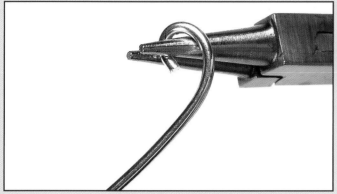
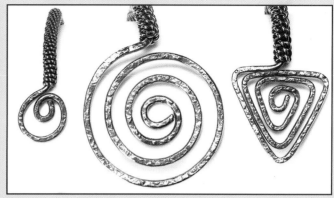

1 **a** Measure your wrist, add 1½ in. (3.8cm) for ease and finishing, then add 10 in. (25cm) to make the cuff with the large spiral design, 8 in. (20cm) to make the triangular design, or 2 in. (5cm) to make the small spiral. Cut a piece of 14-gauge wire to that length.

b Start any of the designs by turning a small loop at the wire's end with roundnose pliers.

2 Refer to these designs as a template for your bracelet or create one of your own. Use your fingers and pliers to bend the wire into the desired shape.

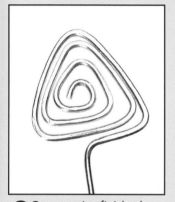
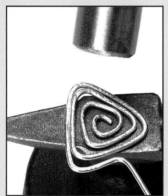
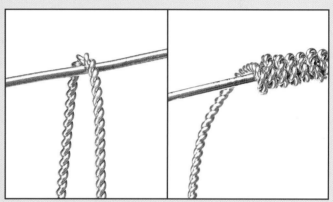

3 Once you've finished shaping the wire, bend the tail at a right angle to the design. (The tail becomes the core for the coiled wire in later steps.)

4 Place the shaped wire on the bench block or anvil. Hammer one side to create a textured finish.

5 Fold the twisted wire in half and rest the fold on the 14-gauge wire tail. Hold the tail and half the twisted wire in one hand. With the other hand, wrap the twisted wire tightly around the core. When you've finished wrapping one end, repeat with the remaining wire. (You'll use approximately 8 in./20cm of twisted wire to make 1 in./2.5cm of coil.) Slide the coil off the core.

6 Place the hammered design on top of your wrist. Use your fingers to shape the core into a loose-fitting cuff. Trim the core wire so it overlaps the design by ½ in. (1.3cm).

7 Slide the coil back on the core. (You may have to straighten the core wire slightly.) Trim the coil so ½ in. of core is exposed.

8 Flatten the wire tip by striking it once or twice with a hammer. Smooth the cut end with a file or emery board. Use roundnose pliers to bend the wire tip into a small hook. Reshape the cuff so the hook catches the outer edge of the wire design.

String a

SOPHISTICATED

fringe

by Andrea Kolasinki Marcinkus

Spin seed beads into lengthy fringe to make a flowing lariat. Though no bead in this piece is larger than 5mm, the vast quantity of seed beads streaming down from your neck will certainly attract attention. Wear the lariat scarf-style, doubled around your neck, or tied loosely, and add matching tassel earrings.

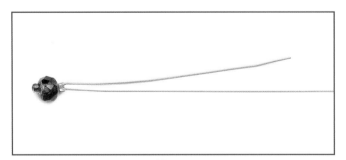

1 **lariat •** Cut ten pieces of flexible beading wire (Basics, p. 7). On one end of each wire, string a microcrimp bead, a 5mm bead, and an 11º seed bead or bugle bead. Go back through the 5mm bead and the microcrimp bead. Leaving a 1-in. (2.5cm) tail, flatten the microcrimp bead (Basics).

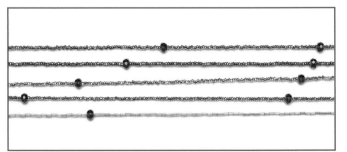

2 Covering the tail of one wire, string 11ºs, interspersing four 5mm beads, until the strand is half the desired length. Repeat to make a total of eight strands.

On another wire, string bugle beads, interspersing four 5mm beads, until the strand is half the desired length. Repeat to make a total of two strands.

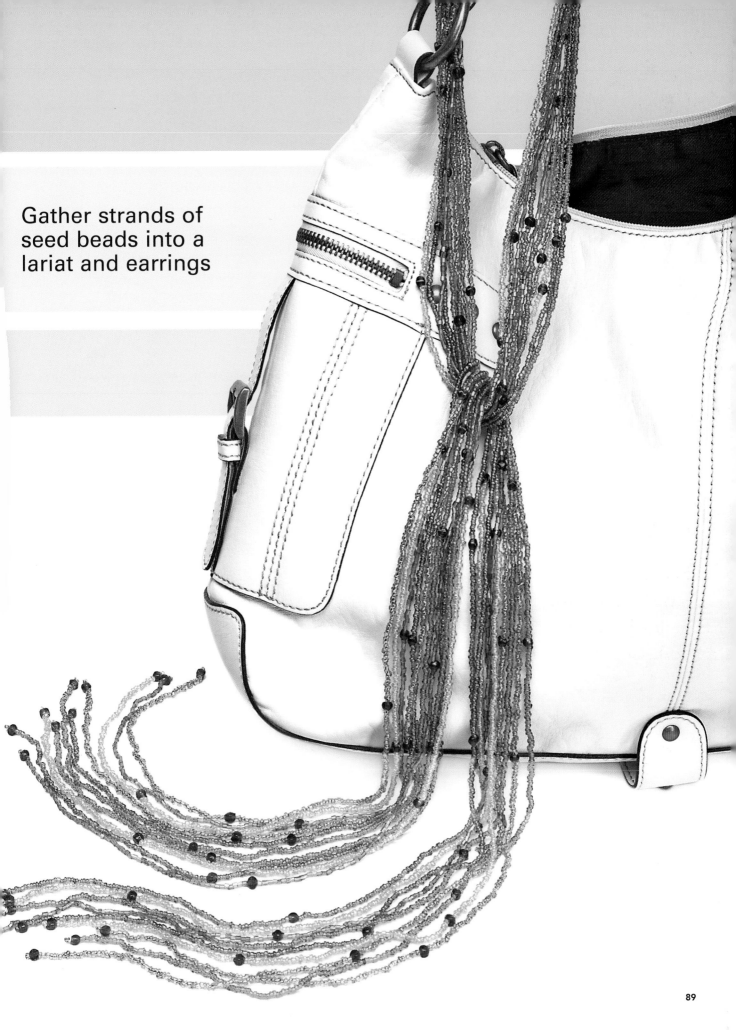

Gather strands of
seed beads into a
lariat and earrings

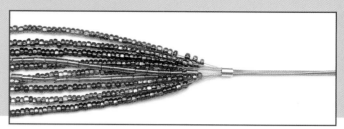

3 Over all ten strands, string a mighty crimp bead. Do not crimp the mighty crimp bead.

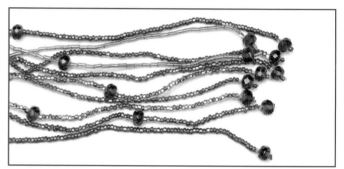

4 **a** On each strand, continue stringing 11ºs or bugle beads, interspersing four 5mm beads, until the strand is within 1 in. (2.5cm) of the desired length.

   b On each strand, string a microcrimp bead, a 5mm bead, and an 11º. Go back through the last few beads strung. Flatten the microcrimp bead.

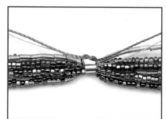 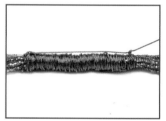

5 Cut a 9-ft. (2.7m) piece of cotton cord and a 9-ft. (2.7m) piece of beading wire. String the cord and the wire through the mighty crimp bead. Tie a surgeon's knot (Basics) around the mighty crimp bead.

6 Wrap one end of the cord back and forth around the gathered strands, extending each side approximately 1 in. (2.5cm) beyond the mighty crimp bead. Leave a 2-in. (5cm) tail. Tie a surgeon's knot around a wrap. Pull the tail across the wraps, and tie a surgeon's knot around a wrap.

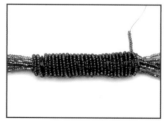 

7 On the beading wire, string 11ºs in a fifth color, leaving a 6-in. (15cm) tail. String a microcrimp bead and flatten it. Wrap the beaded strand around the cord.

8 String the beading wire's tail under a wrap and tie a knot. String the tail under the beaded coil, and tie another knot around a wrap. Trim the excess cord and beading wire. Tuck the ends under the coil.

SupplyList

lariat 52 in. (1.3m)
- **100** 5mm beads
- 20g 3mm bugle beads
- **4** hanks size 11º seed beads in four colors, plus 10g in a fifth color
- flexible beading wire, .010
- 9 ft. (2.7m) cotton cord
- mighty (3mm) crimp bead
- **21** microcrimp (1 x 1mm) beads
- chainnose pliers
- diagonal wire cutters

earrings
- **22** 5mm beads
- 4g 3mm bugle beads
- 12g size 11º seed beads, 3g each of four colors
- flexible beading wire, .010
- 6 in. (15cm) 22-gauge half-hard wire
- **2** 13mm cones
- **30** microcrimp (1 x 1mm) beads
- pair of earring wires
- chainnose pliers
- diagonal wire cutters

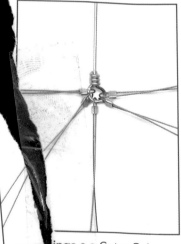

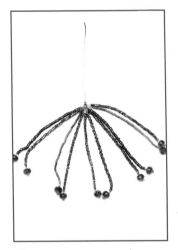

1 earrings • a Cut a 3-in. (7.6cm) piece of 22-gauge wire. Make a wrapped loop on one end. (Basics) Cut five 8-in. (20cm) pieces of beading wire. b Center the loop on one wire. String a microcrimp bead on ends. Flatten the microcrimp bead (Basics). Repeat with the remaining pieces of beading wire.

2 On one wire in each pair of wires, string 3 in. (7.6cm) of 11º seed beads or bugle beads. Repeat on the remaining wire, stringing beads in a different color.

On each end, string a microcrimp bead, a 5mm bead, and an 11º. Go back through the 5mm bead and the last few beads strung. Flatten the microcrimp bead and trim the excess wire.

3 On the 22-gauge wire, string a cone and a 5mm bead. Make a wrapped loop.

4 Open the loop of an earring wire (Basics) and attach the dangle. Close the loop. Make a second earring to match the first.

Sea
CHARMS

A necklace and earrings overflow with a glorious array of pearls, crystals, and gemstones

by Shannon Reeves

Get swept away by this necklace and earrings in colors reminiscent of a day at the beach. Patience is required when attaching these precious bits, but like the cultivation of a beautiful pearl, luxury is the reward. Your opulent collar will enchant all.

1 necklace • Cut a 3-in. (7.6cm) piece of wire. String a top-drilled pearl and make a set of wraps above it (Basics, p. 7). Make the first half of a wrapped loop (Basics) above the wraps. Make 30–40 top-drilled units.

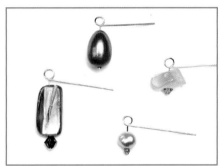

2 String a bead on a head pin. Make the first half of a wrapped loop above the top bead. Make 100–120 bead units. Include small beads or seed beads on some of the units.

3 Determine the finished length of your necklace. (The pink necklace is 15 in./38cm; the blue necklace, 18½ in./ 47cm.) Cut a piece of chain to that length. Attach a top-drilled pearl unit to the center link. Complete the wraps.

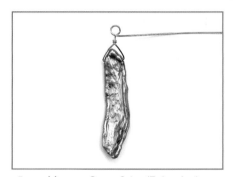

4 On each side of the center unit, continue attaching bead units to the chain until the beaded section is within 6 in. (15cm) of the desired length. Attach two to four bead units per link.

5 Cut a 2½-in. (6.4cm) piece of wire. Make the first half of a wrapped loop on one end. String a 5–6mm bead and make the first half of a wrapped loop above the bead. Repeat to make a second double-loop unit.

6 Check the fit, and trim chain from each end if necessary. On each end, attach a double-loop unit to an end link of chain and half of the clasp. Complete the wraps.

1 earrings • a On a head pin, string one or two beads. Make the first half of a wrapped loop (Basics) above the top bead.

b Cut a 3-in. (7.6cm) piece of wire. String a top-drilled bead and make a set of wraps above it (Basics). Make the first half of a wrapped loop above the wraps. Repeat steps 1a and 1b to make six to nine bead units.

DESIGN GUIDELINES
• Make sure the largest beads you use are long or tube shaped.
• To simplify attaching bead units, attach one type, such as a chip unit, intermittently along the chain. Repeat with another type of bead unit, and so on.
• Allow 6–7 in. (15–18cm) for finishing. Leaving chain open on the sides will create a less bulky, more comfortable necklace.

2 Cut a ½-in. (1.3cm) piece of chain. Open the loop of an earring wire and attach the chain. Close the loop. Attach the longest bead unit to the top link and complete the wraps.

3 Attach the remaining bead units to different links. Make a second earring to match the first.

SupplyList

necklace 15–18½ in. (38–47cm)
• **15–20** 20–30mm stick pearls or mother-of-pearl shards, top drilled
• **15–20** 6–15mm beads, top drilled
• **100–120** 3–20mm crystals, gemstones, and pearls
• 2g size 11º seed beads
• 8–11 ft. (2.4–3.4m) 24-gauge half-hard wire (for top-drilled beads)
• 16–19 in. (41–48cm) chain, 4–5mm links
• **100–120** 2-in. (5cm) 24-gauge head pins
• toggle clasp
• chainnose pliers
• roundnose pliers
• diagonal wire cutters

earrings
• **2** 20–30mm stick pearls or mother-of-pearl shards, top drilled
• **2** 6–15mm beads, top drilled
• **8–14** 3–20mm crystals, gemstones, and pearls
• 6–18 in. (15–46cm) 24-gauge half-hard wire
• 1¼ in. (3.2cm) chain, 4–5mm links
• **8–14** 2-in. (5cm) 24-gauge head pins
• pair of earring wires
• chainnose pliers
• roundnose pliers
• diagonal wire cutters

Contributors

Linda J. Augsburg is Senior Editor/Online for *BeadStyle, Bead&Button,* and *Art Jewelry* magazines. Contact her through Kalmbach Books.

Rupa Balachandar likes to create jewelry that makes a statement, and regularly travels through Asia looking for jewelry components. Contact her via e-mail at info@rupab.com, or her Web site, rupab.com.

Paulette Biedenbender has been beading since 1996 and currently teaches beading throughout the Milwaukee metro area. Contact her via e-mail at h8winters@sbcglobal.net.

Contact **Teri Bienvenue** via her Web site, thebeadingcontessa.com.

Karin Buckingham is the author of *Mostly Metals: A Beginner's Guide to Jewelry Design.* Contact her via her blog, artfulcrafts.blogspot.com.

Contact **Lynne Dixon-Speller** in care of Kalmbach Books.

Contact **Alethia Donathan** via e-mail at dacsbeads@aol.com, or her Web site, dacsbeads.com.

Naomi Fujimoto is Senior Editor of *BeadStyle* magazine and the author of *Cool Jewels: Beading Projects for Teens.* Contact her via e-mail at nfujimoto@beadstyle.com, or visit her blog, cooljewelsnaomi.blogspot.com.

Susan Holland, Graduate Gemologist and co-owner of Alexander-Lee Gallery, has been importing Venetian glass beads and jewelry since 1976. Contact her at 713-789-2564, or visit her Web site, venetianbeads.com.

Louise Jeremich is a New Jersey-based jewelry designer. Her love of free-form design inspires her one-of-a-kind pieces. Contact her via e-mail at jeremichdesigns@aol.com, or visit her Web site, allbentouttashape.etsy.com.

Camilla Jorgensen is a jewelry designer and microbiology student. She lives in Quebec with her husband and their five cats. Contact her via e-mail at info@micalla.com, or visit her Web site, micalla.com.

Eva Kapitany began making jewelry when, instead of prescribing medication, her doctor suggested she find a fun activity to ease her depression. Eva's been depression-free and designing jewelry for seven years. Contact Eva in care of Kalmbach Books.

Anne Nikolai Kloss is a bead artist and instructor from Waukesha, Wis. Contact her via e-mail at annekloss@mac.com.

Jane Konkel is Associate Editor of *BeadStyle* magazine. Her projects can be seen in *Bead Journey*, as well as in other Kalmbach books. Contact her via e-mail at jkonkel@beadstyle.com.

Gail Lannum designs jewelry in Cleveland, Ohio. Contact her via e-mail at moonriverbeads@aol.com, or visit her blog, gaillannum.blogspot.com.

Jewelry designer **Monica Lueder** enjoys adding an elegant flair to her designs. Contact her via e-mail at mdesign@wi.rr.com.

Contact **Andrea Kolasinki Marcinkus** via e-mail at circedesigns@hotmail.com.

Irina Miech is an artist, teacher, and the author of a series of how-to books, including *Metal Clay for Beaders, More Metal Clay for Beaders, Inventive Metal Clay, Beautiful Wire Jewery for Beaders,* and *Metal Clay Rings.* She also oversees Eclectica, a retail bead supply business and classroom studio. Contact Irina at Eclectica, 262-641-0910, or via e-mail at info@eclecticabeads.com.

Polymer clay bead artist **Heather Powers** is the creative force behind Bead Cruise, Bead Week, and the Art Bead Scene. Visit her Web site, humblebeads.com.

Shannon Reeves works at Knot Just Beads in Mobile, Ala., where she designs and sells her jewelry. Shannon, the mother of three boys, believes designing jewelry helps keep her in touch with young women. Contact Shannon via e-mail at thereeves@aol.com.

Karla Schafer is a full-time designer at Auntie's Beads and leads the Karla Kam program, free online instructional beading videos. Contact Karla via e-mail at karla@auntiesbeads.com, or visit auntiesbeads.com.

Arlene Schreiber graduated from Michigan State University, where she studied graphic design and fine arts. Arlene has been beading for the last 10 years and finds that inspiration comes from her strong sense of color. Contact her via e-mail at ams2fm@comcast.net.

Brenda Schweder is the author of the books *Junk to Jewelry* and *Vintage Redux* and is a frequent contributor to *BeadStyle, Bead&Button*, and *Art Jewelry* magazines. Contact her via e-mail at b@brendaschweder.com, or visit her Web site, brendaschweder.com.

Beautiful beads provide plenty of inspiration for **Juliana Thaens**. Contact her via e-mail at julianascreations@yahoo.com, or her Web sites, julianascreations.etsy.com and julianascreations.com.

Contact **Stacie Thompson** in care of Kalmbach Books.

Susan Tobias is a full-time artist who creates her own jewelry in Hartland, Wis. Contact Susan via e-mail at dktobias@prodigy.net.

Wendy Witchner is a wire and metal jewelry artist who travels the United States in her motor home to sell her creations at art shows. Her work is also available at select galleries. Visit her Web site, wendywitchner-jewelry.com.

Jean Yates, of Westchester County, N.Y., is the author of a wire-working book titled *Links* and enjoys creating beading tutorials. Her specialty is wirework integrating polymer and lampworked beads. Visit her at prettykittydogmoonjewelry.com, or prettykittydogmoonjewelry.blogspot.com.

Get international
flair from fashionable jewelry designs

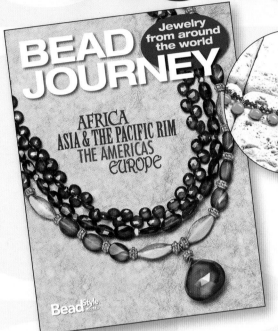

Twenty-five projects from the *BeadStyle Around the World* special issue and eight new projects showcase beads and jewelry styles from all over the globe. The step-by-step photos, instructions and projects from Asia and the Pacific Rim, Africa, Europe, and the Americas, make this an easy-to-follow and unique beading guide with international inspiration. 96 pages.

62670 • $19.95

Compiled by the editors of *Bead&Button* magazine, *Chic&Easy Beading* presents 100 stylish and easy-to-make jewelry designs and variations. Beautiful photos and detailed instructions make this book suitable for both beginning and advanced bead artists. 144 pages.

12265 • $21.95

Compiled from the pages of *Chic&Easy Beading*, *Bead&Button*, and *BeadStyle* this book showcases 100 fabulous jewelry projects, an illustrated basic techniques section, and more. Achieving professional jewelry results can really be fast and fun. 144 pages.

62253 • $21.95

Get more of what made the first two *Chic&Easy Beading* volumes great: simple stringing and basic weaving projects that result in fashionable and wearable necklaces, bracelets, and earrings. 144 pages.

62779 • $21.95